Andrew Friend & Andy M

Slump City

The Politics of Mass Unemployment

Pluto Press

Second impression 1982
First published 1981 by Pluto Press Limited,
The Works, 105A Torriano Avenue, London NW5 2RX

Copyright © Andrew Friend and Andy Metcalf 1981

ISBN 0 86104 342 1

Cover photograph by Mike Goldwater
Cover design by Terry Seago

Photoset by Promenade Graphics Limited, Cheltenham
Printed and bound in Great Britain at
The Camelot Press Limited, Southampton

Acknowledgements

At the outset this book was going to be a very different product, using pictures and fiction as well as much more interview material. In those early days Lauren Dale and Cathy Blackie worked closely with us as photographers and Anna Douglas helped us with the interviews. Those we interviewed provided experiences which have guided the book during its lengthy evolution. The final outcome owes a lot to all of them. Since then, both the struggle to locate local events in a wider framework and the economics of publishing have pushed the project towards its present format. At each stage many people have been generous with their encouragement and gentle with their criticism—both have been crucial. We would like to thank everybody who has commented on the various drafts and in particular want to mention Altheia Jones-Lecointe, Annie Brackx, Bob Rowthorn, Charlie Foreman, Cynthia Cockburn, Gustav Fahrenkrog, John Wilkinson, Mike Edwards, Mike Reid, Paul Crane, Richard Kuper, Stuart Speedon, Trevor Evans and Tony Bogues. The shortcomings are down to us.

Andy Metcalf's son Ben supplied a steady stream of distraction, drawings and arguments. Our men's groups, Susie Orbach, Joe Schwartz and other close friends helped and supported us through both the good and the bad times. Gillian Slovo and Luise Eichenbaum gave freely of their love and care.

Andrew Friend
Andy Metcalf

Contents

Introduction

10 November 1980: Unemployment in Britain could soar to almost four million by 1985 if the Government sticks to its present public spending plans. In a survey of almost unrelieved gloom the Cambridge Econometrics Group today warns that, even if public spending cuts are restrained, there will still be 3.5 million out of work by the middle of the present decade. *The Guardian*.

14 August 1977: The streets of Lewisham in South-East London became a bloody battleground yesterday as blacks and left-wing protestors clashed with police and about one thousand National Front marchers. It was London's worst street violence since the war. *The Sunday Times*.

Parliament, 6 April 1977: Mr Peter Shore, Secretary of State for the Environment, outlined a six point plan for improving inner city areas. Over the past decade, inner cities have suffered a massive and disproportionate loss of jobs and a major exodus of population. Substantial ethnic minorities in some cities have added an extra dimension of difficulty. The old problems of poor housing . . . have still to be overcome; but in many areas they have been joined by new problems of high unemployment, decay and dereliction. *The Guardian*.

By the end of 1976, when we started work on this book, it was already clear that 'decay and dereliction' across significant tracts of Britain's major cities were creating new problems of social and political control for the state. The sharp rise in unemployment that had followed on from the 1974-75 recession had been particularly pronounced in what now became known as 'the inner city'. The media began to fasten attention on particular groups such as the long-term unemployed, the low paid, isolated old people and black and white working class youth. The government responded by producing a whole new range of 'inner city policies'. At the same time, a series of confrontations in the big cities saw a marked growth in the use of police power. In fact the 'inner cities'—where social and economic problems appeared particularly entrenched—were the scene of some of the most intense conflicts during the middle years of the Labour government.

During this period Labour succeeded in checking the industrial militancy that had brought down the previous Conservative administration. But in the winter of 1978-79 the Labour government's strategy of containment collapsed. Since then, the particular problems facing the state in the inner urban areas have been partially eclipsed, as the quickening pace of deindustrialisation has created new concentrations of unemployment beyond those areas that were singled out as blackspots in the mid-seventies. With unemployment rising steeply, the crisis of social and political control generated by concentrations of people existing on the margins of society is set to become both more widespread and more intense.

It is a central concern of this book to explore how and why these concentrations occur, their class composition and their significance for the working class on the one hand and the state on the other. This chapter begins the investigation by looking at why the state was forced to formulate a new response to conditions in the inner city, and at the impact the election of a Tory government had on that response. It then outlines our approach to the 'inner city problem' and introduces some of the concepts used in the rest of the book.

The Labour government's inner city problem

Over 200,000 people attended the three days of the 1976 Notting Hill Carnival. The crowds were overwhelmingly black. The previous year there had been 200 police on hand, but that year there were 1,600. During the weekend the tension between the revellers and the police became electric and finally on the last night it exploded. Street battles between young blacks and the police broke out and clashes continued for several hours. Cars were burnt, heads were broken and the police made repeated charges. The next day's newspapers carried photos of sacked shops and their editorials made direct comparisons with the looting and burning that had occurred in American cities during the sixties. Controversy followed as many of the papers—including the *Financial Times*—claimed that it was the heavy-handed policing that had caused the outbreak of violence. 'There are not going to be any no-go areas in London', was the reply from the Commissioner of Metropolitan Police.

Three weeks later, in September 1976, the Secretary of State for the Environment announced that the government was embarking on a major policy review, designed to halt urban decay. 'Twentieth century civilisation has been built around cities,' he said, 'if cities fail, so to a large extent does our society.' In the next few months, as reports on inner city job losses, unemployment and vandalism rolled off the presses, the outlines of a new policy package emerged. Development resources were to be switched from outer areas back into the central districts of the conurbations through a general redistribution of central government grants and a cut-back in the New Town development programme. The special 'urban aid' programme, started in the late sixties, would be expanded: central government would enter into a number of 'partnerships' with local authorities in the most run-down inner city areas; a new law would allow local authorities to entice industry back into their patches by offering incentives; special attention would be paid to protecting the interests of small businesses in the cities.

The succession of policy statements created a surface impression of great and meaningful activity; but even as they did, a series of dramatic clashes in the major conurbations underlined the fact that events in Britain's cities were increasingly presenting the government with problems of public order not seen in mainland Britain since the thirties. The problems, beginning with the Carnival in 1976, continued with mass police mobilisations directed against demonstrations opposing National Front activities in Manchester and Wood Green, North London. There were also scenes of mass disorder in North-West London outside a film processing plant called Grunwicks—a small business of the very type that government policies were now supposed to encourage. A strike had been going on there for nine months when the Trades Council started to organise mass pickets in support of the immigrant workers fighting for union recognition. Throughout the month of July 1977 there was fierce fighting between police and pickets, but, despite the hundreds of arrests, support continued to grow in the labour movement and the mass pickets swelled. Once again the Metropolitan Police Commissioner was faced with the issue of deciding who was going to control the streets. Barely two weeks after government pressure on the trade union hierarchy had succeeded in getting the regular mass pickets called off, the street battles in Lewisham took place. The following week the events at Lewisham were repeated when the National Front held a by-election meeting at Ladywood in Birmingham. By now it was becoming increasingly difficult to put the disturbances down to small groups of troublemakers; a chorus of protest from unexpected quarters was greeting the police handling of the confrontations. There was a growing realisation that the numbers involved were large and the 'troublemakers' were not isolated. At the Carnival, the crowds had, in the main, supported black youth against the police; outside Grunwicks, post office workers and miners had supported immigrant workers, many of whom were women. After Ladywood *The Guardian* commented that: 'the new and dangerous element today is the conjunction of economic recession, mass unemployment—especially among the young and unskilled—and the alienation of our young black citizens.'

The fear that changes in the social and economic organisation of British society were marginalising sections of the urban working class had guided the special urban programmes since the late sixties. Now official references to the existence of the urban poor became more frequent. The government Housing Minister linked what he called 'a spreading sickness in our society' to the fate of four million people living in a decaying environment. Tory ex-Secretary of State for the Environment, Peter Walker was more explicit: 'The problem of our inner cities is caused by the concentration of people living on the economic and social margins of society. This concentration is increasing . . . The problem of the inner city is the most serious social problem facing British Government.' Looking back over a file of ministerial speeches from this period, we can see this fear of the urban poor lurking behind ritual references to the 'unbalanced nature of the migration' encouraged by government dispersal policies, the jargonistic asides about 'social bi-polarisation' and the sense of 'collective deprivation' felt by people living in areas of industrial decline.

This fear is not new in Britain. In the nineteenth century and particularly in London, fear of the massed urban poor influenced a whole range of new social policies and government interventions. The threat of disorder in the capital became particularly acute because of the impact of the industrial revolution on London's economy. Until then, London had been a major manufacturing centre as well as Britain's premier port and capital city. But as the old craft industries were challenged by northern factories, and as heavy industry closed down to be resited on cheaper land near to coalfields, a growing proportion of the city's burgeoning population became dependent on casual or seasonal employment. In the 1850s Mayhew calculated that: 'out of the 4.5 million people who have to depend on their industry for the livelihood of themselves and their families, there is barely sufficient work for the regular employment of half our labourers, so that only 1.5 million are fully and constantly employed, while 1.5 million are employed only half their time and the remaining 1.5 million wholly unemployed.'[1] This estimate now appears to be exaggerated, but even if we halve Mayhew's figures we are still left with a 'casual residuum' numbering a million. Small wonder then that when the urban poor took to demonstrations, riots and looting, they terrified the upper and middle classes.[2] Much urban development during this period, from the road widening schemes which broke up the old central slums to the initiation of public drainage schemes and the foundation of the police force to protect upper class residential districts, can be traced to the governing classes' fear of the massed urban poor.

Over the past fifteen years, as high levels of unemployment have returned to areas of many big cities, this old fear has reappeared in modern forms. Its revival was specifically precipitated by the revolt in the black ghettoes of the USA during the mid-sixties. During 1964 this revolt first hit the headlines when New York, New Jersey, Philadelphia and Chicago saw attacks on police stations, the firing of whole neighbourhoods and the sacking of large white-owned shops. The following summer Watts erupted into weeks of street battles and in July 1967 the long hot summers seemed to reach a crescendo with Detroit in flames and under army occupation—in that month alone there had been uprisings in forty cities with gun battles becoming a standard feature of black–police relations. When Martin Luther King—effective leader of the pacifist wing of the black struggle—was assassinated less than a year later, mass rioting broke out simultaneously in 125 cities across 29 states. Fifty-three thousand troops were deployed, over twenty-one thousand people were arrested and the number killed in repressing the revolt exceeded the number of US combat deaths in an average week at the height of the Vietnam war.[3] The prelude to this period had seen the black population of the northern and western cities grow considerably as big business moved in on southern agriculture, displacing black workers from the land. From the end of the war up to 1965, some four million black people left the land for the cities, only to find themselves excluded from both the economic and the political structures of the old cities.

As the numbers of blacks in the cities grew, members of the white middle classes speeded up their departure plans for the suburban dormitories. In the neighbourhoods bordering on the black areas racism assumed a more overt form, as conflicts arose over the allocation of public resources. In nearly all the large cities white residents' groups consistently and vocally opposed public housing projects that favoured blacks and fought against the effective desegregation of schools. Equally consistently, city governments pursued policies reflecting the attitudes of the voting blocs that had elected them, with the result that conditions in the ghettoes worsened as overcrowding intensified. During the fifties welfare administrations contrived ways of withholding benefits from new arrivals, while in many cities the general public housing programme virtually ceased as 'urban renewal' was consciously used to remove blacks from areas of the city that had become racially mixed.

The black population of the great American cities was marginalised economically as well as politically. They found work hard to get as the manufacturing industry closed down to resite elsewhere and racial barriers continued to bar them from those areas of employment with growing payrolls—the head office, state and financial service sectors. Unemployment began to rise—especially amongst black youth. In 1948, 7.6 per cent of non-white male teenagers were unemployed—by 1963 the figure had risen to 25.4 per cent nationally, while in areas like Harlem in New York the figure was over 50 per cent. In rural areas unemployment and underemployment had been part of a pattern of subsistence living; but being without a job on the streets of the richest cities of the world was quite another matter.

The budding rebellion of black and hispanic youth drew sustenance from the militant struggle for civil rights which was waged in the south from 1960 onwards. Eventually the black power movement arose from within this struggle to reach deep into the black working class. At the same time as this was occurring, growing resistance to the Vietnam war was rocking American society as more and more people became radicalised by the consequences of the incredible military intransigence of a tiny and despised Asian nation. It was the combination of all these events which was reponsible for the most serious internal upheavals America had experienced for nearly forty years.

In Britain during the sixties it was only Northern Ireland that presented the state with an immediate threat of mass disorder. This is not to say that Britain's Labour government was unconcerned about conditions within its mainland cities at this time. Starting in the early sixties, a series of government enquiries into a wide range of subjects—from London's housing to primary education, social services and the problems of children and young persons—had all pointed their finger to islands of 'deprivation' in the working class districts of Britain's older industrial cities. Here, bad housing, poor educational facilities, poverty and juvenile crime were found to go hand in hand.[5] The reports spotlighted the fact that the normal processes of the welfare state were having little impact on these 'pockets of deprivation'. More alarming to the government was the uncanny resemblance of their findings to the problems of crime, vandalism and dependence on welfare which had been brought to light in the early 1960s in the US ghettoes.

As the ghetto uprisings came to a climax in 1968, the British government was becoming aware of growing militancy within the black working class, stirred up by events across the Atlantic and increasingly confident in its rejection of second class citizenship. With the emergence of new forms of opposition, the government was also coming under pressure to make an initiative in the urban arena from other directions. Pressure groups external to the main political parties—concentrating on single issues such as homelessness and 'underprivileged' children—attempted to mobilise public opinion in favour of extended welfare policies. In the inner cities themselves, new and more direct forms of opposition began to gain ground. Homelessness rose precipitously as the post-war slum clearance programmes reached a climax—in response, small groups employed the tactics of squatting empty property. Such 'direct action' came to be widely used by various groups opposing local authority plans or pushing for better services. However, despite the pressure for a new initiative, government policy was hamstrung by the continuing stagnation of the British economy and growing demands to encourage private enterprise and cut back on the rate of growth in social spending.

In 1968 the government tried to resolve these contradictory demands by announcing the Urban Programme, and then providing it with minimal funding. As the CDP pamphlet *Gilding the Ghetto* points out: 'The money made available for Urban Aid was not an extra government grant, but money already existing in the rate support grant, which was taken out of the general allocation and put into the special grant category.'

Control over the major part of this programme was given to the Home Office, the ministry responsible for law and order. This phase of state policy towards the older working class areas has been extensively examined elsewhere;[6] here we simply want to pick up three strands common to this first generation of urban programmes. A major aim behind all the projects set up at this time was to bid for the consent of the governed in areas with the highest concentration of urban poor. Thus councils of community relations were set up in areas with large immigrant populations in an attempt to vocalise the discontent of minorities and channel it into governable forms. Similarly, community groups and pressure organisations were often funded and a parallel emphasis on public 'participation' crept into many areas of local government activity. A second underlying theme that can be traced through the programmes is the attempt to bolster or implant elements of community self-help into areas where the traditional package of social services and the forces of law and order were failing to cope. The shoring up of crumbling family units was seen as particularly important. Further public expense, entailed by taking kids into care, or the costs of vandalism and juvenile crime, would be avoided by encouraging more stable and responsible family units. The importance of family stability was stressed by the then fashionable sociological explanations of urban poverty—namely that it was a problem of people caught in 'cycles of deprivation', rather than a result of structural economic change. As a Home Office press release put it on 16 July 1969:

> Ill health—financial difficulties—children suffering from deprivation—consequent delinquency—inability of the children to adjust to adult life—unstable marriages—emotional problems—ill health and the cycle begins again.

Finally there was a strong tendency to explain the persistence of urban poverty as arising from the wrong mix of policies and lack of co-ordination between different central and local government departments. This was reinforced when new restrictions on rises in public expenditure precluded an expansion of existing service.

Since the start of this first generation of urban programmes the decay of the inner cities has intensified. These initiatives proved incapable of containing and safely channelling the anger of the urban poor because they left the dynamic of economic decay absolutely untouched. Throughout the sixties and into the seventies the inner urban areas suffered from a flight of industrial jobs—for example, between 1966 and 1971 manufacturing employment declined by 20 per cent in Manchester and by 18 per cent in Inner London.[7] Worse was to follow as the climate of slowing growth that had governed economic activity during the late sixties gave way to deep recession in 1974—all the more powerful

14

because it embraced all the central capitalist economies simultaneously. This recession brought bankruptcy and merger, as competition for markets became frantic. It quickened the pace of industrial change and hastened the death of inefficient firms in the inner city, and the merger of efficient firms which then uprooted to New Towns and suburban sites. Recession has brought with it a level of unemployment unprecedented in the post-war period—concentrated in the old regions of industrial decline and the new zones of urban decay. Poplar, in London's East End, had an unemployment rate of 13.3 per cent in September 1976—over double the national average; in the same month unemployment among active men in the Liverpool 7 and 8 districts was running at 33 per cent.

The working class of the inner cities has become one of the main bearers of the burdens and costs of the recession. Economic crisis has intensified the contradictory demands on government which were already bearing down on it in the late sixties. On an international scale, the 1974-75 recession prompted governments to bail out failing firms, allow corporations to escape their tax demands and increase incentives, in order to underwrite profits and ward off the collapse of major enterprises. The Labour government responded to the depth of the economic crisis by making drastic cuts in social public expenditure in order to provide public funds for the industrial sector. This transfer of state aid was at the core of the last government's 'industrial strategy'. And the cut-backs in social spending, introduced in 1976-77, hit hardest at the unemployed, the old, disabled, chronically sick, those in bad housing conditions and those on the receiving end of rundown services.

In 1977 the Labour government took a new initiative with its inner city policy, centering on the 'partnership programmes', including special allocation of £100 million a year to a number of older working class areas. Unfortunately it was labouring under the impact of a major contradiction from its inception. While one arm of the government was administering the inner city programmes, the other was beginning to cut social spending and providing financial backing and encouragement for a restructuring of industry which would exacerbate the flight of productive capital from these areas. It was, and was seen to be, pitifully inadequate: 'barely enough to put tinsel in the window'. Nevertheless Labour's inner city programme represented a genuine break with the first generation of urban policies. The thrust of the new policies was not directed at 'problem families', the 'lack of community' and the need for public participation, but at reversing the flight of industry and consequent economic deline. The sheer scope of this decline, the degree of unemployment in the inner cities, meant that it was no longer plausible to ascribe the problems of the unemployed to 'cycles of deprivation'.

The second generation of urban programmes concentrated on providing finance and legal powers to local authorities to entice back industry; they focused on the seven partnership areas of Liverpool, Manchester/Salford, Birmingham, Newcastle/Gateshead, London Docklands, Hackney/Islington, and Lambeth. These are the areas where central government, in association with local authorities, has spent over 70 per cent of the total inner city programme's budget. Funds were made available to improve the industrial infrastructure, to prepare advance factory sites, to grant rent-free periods to incoming firms and provide them with other financial assistance. Outside of the partnership areas, local authorities in 14 other districts and boroughs received powers to assist the regeneration of local industry. Furthermore all the 'job-creation' programmes introduced in reaction to youth employment were instructed to have an inner city bias and all government departments were exhorted to adopt 'inner city perspectives'.

The whole programme was based on the premise that state-provided incentives could counterbalance the factors which led to firms leaving the inner city in the first place. The same premise underlay the whole of post-war regional policy and, as we shall see later, the inner city programmes are only the failed tools of regional policy, repolished. In the last ten years they have failed to prevent the re-emergence of high levels of unemployment and poverty in the old depressed regions; and they are failing today in the inner cities. Their inefficacy does not stem primarily from the low level of funding, but, as we shall show in Chapter 3, from the inherent inability of the British (or any other capitalist) state to smooth out the uneven development that follows from the capitalist pursuit of profit. The partnership programmes have not reversed the dynamic of decay, and unemployment has continued to rise faster, and respond less readily to cyclical recovery in inner urban areas than elsewhere (see Chapter 4 below). Ironically, far from providing a new beginning in these areas, much of the partnership funding was used to make up for the cuts in capital spending programmes imposed after 1976 and help limit the massive rate rises that became necessary to maintain even a reduced level of services in these areas.

The contradiction between special action to rebuild the inner urban areas and the imperatives of industrial restructuring and maintaining profitability became even more acute with the election of the Tory government in 1979. Given the public emphasis on rolling back the boundaries of the welfare state in order to create a free market economy fired by enterprise and initiative, less has been heard about the partnership programmes. Nevertheless, despite the fact that spending has declined in real terms, the special urban programme remains largely intact. The Tories have even come up with their own urban initiatives. The setting up of New Town style Urban Development Corporations to steer the development of London and Liverpool docklands follows in the mould of previous tinkering with the mix of policies, but has the advantage of stripping away elements of local democratic control over the redevelopment process. The other major innovation has been the setting up of 'enterprise zones' in the older urban areas, where planning regulations have been minimised and tax exemptions have been granted to existing and incoming companies. But the most significant development in government policy towards these areas has not been anything that carries the urban label, but rather Thatcher's statement soon after coming into office that 'deprived inner city areas cannot expect to escape public spending cuts.'

In the first eighteen months of the Tory government there have been several major rounds of public spending cuts. In June 1979, £1.5 billion was cut from the £65 billion budget for 1979-80 inherited from the previous administration. Four months later £3.5 billion was cut from the budget for 1980-81. This coincided with the publication of plans for state spending up to 1983-84, which not only provided for a further decline of £3 billion in gross annual total expenditure, but also for a redistribution of resources between programmes. Thus substantial increases in defence and law and order spending have been balanced against very severe real cuts in expenditure on housing, health, education and social services. Continuing a trend begun under Labour, housing has been severely hit—in 1974-75 total housing expenditure was over £7.1 billion, by 1979-80 it had fallen to £5.1 billion, and according to Tory plans will have fallen to £2.8 billion by 1983-84. (All figures in this paragraph are at 1979 survey prices). At the time of writing a third round of spending cuts, designed to keep government spending within these overall targets, appears to be in preparation—large rises in unemployment, pushing up social security spending, and the effects of the recession on the nationalised industries have forced these further measures. Given previous experience, we can expect the government's 'welfare state' activities to once again suffer disproportionately.

There are two major reasons why the impact of these cuts is particularly severe in the older working class areas. Firstly, a high proportion of the population in inner city areas are either dependent on services which will decline—the old and chronically sick, single parents, unemployed youth—or work in the public services, which are being cut and therefore either shedding or no longer recruiting labour. Second, the government has reversed the Labour administration's policy of tilting the rate support grant settlement towards the big cities and shown itself more than ready to axe special urban spending and single out inner city authorities in its battle to force down local government expenditure.

Although there are differences between the previous and the present government's policies towards the inner cities, there is also much continuity. Since the 1976 IMF deal, the Labour government had been pursuing a muted monetarist policy with all the restrictions on public spending that implied. Its commitment to operating within a capitalist framework had, at a time of crisis, the consequence of forcing sections of the working class to take a reduction in their standard of living. The thrust of capitalist development in the UK in the seventies had been altered very little by regional and inner city programmes, and when this caused serious problems of social order the Labour Cabinet backed the police forces' handling of them to the full. Thatcher's monetarism is a more rigorous application of Healey's brand. Although it has kept the tinsel of the inner city programmes in the window, the house has continued to disintegrate around it.

Differences do exist however. The Labour Party in government, confronted by social crisis in areas which traditionally supported it at the polls, was forced to come to terms with the underlying decline of the inner area economies. It presented this decline as the result of the wrong combination of policies. Over and over again, Labour's ministerial statements stressed the mistakes of government population dispersal policies, the problems caused by the industrial development certificate system, the blight of bureaucratic inertia etc. At the same time they held out totally unrealistic hopes that a little spending here, more sensitive planning there, could create an environment where growth would resume to the mutual advantage of both investors and the inner urban working class. By developing the partnership programmes, they reinforced the illusion that the state could control uneven development in a mixed economy and mystified the nature of the changes that had overtaken the inner areas.

The Tories for their part have a more hard-headed approach: they realise that a revival of capitalist growth in these areas depends on creating conditions in which labour can be more profitably exploited by capital. Thus they think in terms of enterprise zones where planning, environmental and even health and safety regulations can be relaxed. They believe that benefits must rise less than the inflation rate, that earnings-related unemployment benefit should go and that social security should be withheld from people with small amounts of savings or those who have received redundancy payments. All these measures are designed to increase the incentive for people to accept jobs with low pay and bad conditions that they would not have previously considered taking. In areas of already high unemployment, they may begin to create an environment within which entrepreneurs will more easily be able to exploit the oversupply of labour.

Dividing the working class

The May 1979 general election highlighted the significant differences of political outlook and perceptions of material self-interest that exist between the relatively secure and prosperous layers of the working class on the one hand, and those who exist on low incomes, work in threatened jobs and live in less prosperous regions and areas on the other. It is clear that a determined effort to exploit these differences and prise open this division within the working class electorate was a crucial part of the Conservative campaign. The strategy embraced a crude and unashamed attempt to find scapegoats for the crisis within the working class: thus militant trade unionists were branded 'wreckers', the recipients of welfare were labelled 'scroungers' and immigrants were presented as threatening 'aliens'. But it also included a carefully judged appeal to the material interests of better-off working class households. Thus the Tory proposals to reduce income tax and cut public expenditure not only accorded with monetarist economic theory, but also appealed directly to skilled manual and non-manual wage earners, and families whose standard of living was not directly dependent on the 'welfare state' activities of central and local government. Similarly, the Conservative promise to 'roll back the boundaries of the state' accorded with the dominant ruling class assessment of its own self-interest. But it also fed off the inadequacy of the services provided by the state and gained ideological force from the alienation that most people feel when they come into personal contact with even the most benign aspects of the state apparatus.

A very clear example of this was the Conservative promise to sell public sector housing to sitting tenants at up to 50 per cent off market valuation. This pledge was clearly aimed at families with above average regular incomes living in the public sector, who—like all tenants—had seen rents soar over the previous three years, while the rise in property values was once again giving very substantial financial rewards to owner-occupiers. The Tories realised that nobody would buy in the public sector slums of today or tomorrow, and that selling off the best public housing would further hamper local authorities seeking to meet the housing aspirations of remaining tenants and those on the waiting list. They also realised that if better-off council tenants could be enticed out of the sector then the difference between public sector renting and owner occupation would become an even more marked and concrete expression of the very division in the working class they were, and are, seeking to exploit. Such developments are now also possible in areas like education and health care. The potential for their encouragement became very clear soon after the election when the Electrical Electronic Telecommunication and Plumbing Union announced (to a chorus of TUC protest) that it had accepted a private health insurance scheme as part of a wages deal concluded on behalf of some of its members.

Throughout the election campaign the Conservatives exploited the popular association between 'socialism' and the existing role of the state as a provider of inadequate services. They coupled this with an insistence that the way out of the crisis lay in forcing individuals and enterprises to brave the storms of a freer market economy. The Labour Party's appeal to the electorate was almost solely based on the proposition that it was the lesser of two evils. Thus they sought to highlight the consequences of Conservative policies for regions of high unemployment, for those working in less profitable sectors and those dependent on services provided by the state. This was sufficient to rally some support in Scotland and the North of England but in the Midlands and the South-East the Conservatives gained heavily in the more prosperous working class suburbs. And some of the largest swings to the Tories occurred in the suburban but predominantly working class constituencies to the East of London. However, in London's inner urban areas, where it had seemed the National Front might make electoral headway two years previously, Labour retained most of its seats and the swing to the Conservatives was small. By and large, this was true for most inner urban constituencies.

The results of the 1979 general election did reflect—however crudely—a division in the working class. Since then the Tories have pursued fiscal and monetary policies which, together with renewed recession, have led to a sharp rise in both overall and long-term unemployment. By seeking to use mass unemployment as a drill sergeant for disciplining the working class as a whole they have hardened up the division. This has been reinforced by changes in the field of employment, immigration and housing law.

This division is not, of course, the creation of successful Conservative political strategy or propaganda. The electoral success of the right was built on, and in turn itself deepened, a long-standing breach within the working class that can be traced back at least as far as the gulf that existed between the 'rough' and 'respectable' working class in nineteenth century Britain. Although such a division has always existed, it has assumed different significance at different points in time. This has happened when the uneven development of the capitalist economy has swollen or reduced the numbers living on the margins of society and as the interaction of uneven development and the changing balance of class forces has acted either to unite or fragment the working class as a whole.

We believe that it is only within this perspective—of changing class relationships and the uneven development of the capitalist system—that a useful understanding of the events and trends associated with 'the inner city problem' or 'urban crisis' can be evolved.

There is no 'inner city problem'

When the problem of the inner city first came to the fore in the mid-seventies, the glib comparisons the media were so fond of making between British and North American cities reinforced the idea that it is cities which are somehow the root cause of unemployment, vandalism, mugging, heroin addiction, etc. In 1976 political circumstances forced the Labour administration to respond to the 'inner city problem' at the economic level and this did to some extent shift public attention towards the effects of economic change in particular areas. But by presenting local situations as stemming solely from the problems peculiar to local areas the media have once again been able to obscure the real forces at work. The growth of urban studies as an academic discipline has backed this up in the form of an analysis which claims that cities can be studied as closed systems. The dominant schools of thought in urban sociology all pose the urban as something distinctive and specific in modern society and many marxists have adopted a similar perspective. But, rather than regarding cities solely in terms of their economic structure and *function*, we would assert that the crucial feature of modern British urban life is the way their economic, social and political *relations* are being transformed through the uneven development of the whole of British society. So in our view there is no inner city problem that can be understood outside of the uneven development of the capitalist system as a whole. This is not to say that the nature and quality of social relations is identical in a big city, new town or village. But the differences between social life in these settings have become relatively slight, for the development of capitalism has industrialised agricultural production and abolished the great divide between town and country, worker and peasant.

What makes the inner city zones of great conurbations stand out from other urban and rural areas is that the burden of restructuring the economy is falling with disproportionate weight on the working class of the older urban areas. As this has occurred, so sections of this inner city working class have been marginalised from the dominant sectors of the economy and either become dependent on social security or found themselves obliged to work in the worst paid reaches of the economy. Now such a process at the level of the economy does not, of itself, produce rebellion. The latter has been assured by the development in some fractions of the urban working class of a consciousness of oppression and strains of resistance which have grown in strength as the process of marginalisation has proceeded apace. The 'urban crisis' has become a crisis for the state because of the formation and concentration of marginalised fractions of the urban working class in the inner cities—fractions who have not borne the consequences of this development passively (See Chapter 6 below).

When we use the term marginalised we do not want to give credence to Home Office notions of 'cycles of deprivation' or 'personal inadequacy'. Neither do we want to convey the idea that these people do not have an economic role within the capitalist mode of production. Not only are they essential to the survival of certain branches of production, but they are also part of a great army of the unemployed which has an undeniable braking effect on the militancy of the employed sections of the working class. Nor, as we have already made clear, have they been swept beyond the boundaries of class struggle. Indeed, we will be arguing that because of the way the working class has been recomposed in the post-war period, the relationship of those who have been marginalised to the rest of the working class and to the state, is of critical political importance during the current phase of stagnation.

Marx, in analysing the uneven growth of industrial capitalism in nineteenth century Britain, classified all those workers who could find no foothold in the central sectors of the production process as constituting a surplus population. We are going to return to this concept, not out of any religious reverence for Marx's writings, but because his analysis, suitably modified for the present day, seems to us to be by far the most precise and clear way of analysing one element of the class structure as it is evolving in urban Britain. Marx grouped together into the surplus population all those who were partially or wholly unemployed, those excluded from work by reasons of age, disability and so on, and those working in certain special branches of production. In doing so, he identified four categories of the surplus population permanently present in nineteenth century Britain.

First was a group of adult male workers who had been employed as child and juvenile labourers 'up to the age of maturity but not beyond. Once they reach maturity, only a very small number continue to find employment in the same branches of industry, while the majority are regularly dismissed.'[8] The second (or latent) form of the surplus population was composed of agricultural workers on the point of leaving the land who were about to join the urban or manufacturing proletariat. The third group Marx calls the stagnant population: 'This forms a part of the active labour army, but with extremely irregular employment . . . Its conditions of life sink below the average normal level of the working class, and it is precisely this which makes it a broad foundation for special branches of capitalist exploitation. It is characterised by a maximum of working time and a minimum of wages.'[9] The final stratum of the relative surplus population 'dwells in the sphere of pauperism' and includes orphans, those unable to work, the old, the disabled, and widows.

Two of these categories are directly applicable today. Special branches of production characterised by 'a maximum working time and a minimum of wages' are still very much with us.

Included in this category are those working in the bottom reaches of the 'black economy' outside the tax system, those in the labour-intensive sweated occupations, homeworkers, and those working on the lowest rungs of the service industries in catering, hotels, tourism etc. So too is pauperism—given modern form by the welfare state. It comprises all those living in households whose only source of income is long-term benefits. It therefore includes a majority of the old, the chronically sick, and those single parents excluded from the mainstream labour market because of childcare responsibilities.

With the eradication of smallholders, peasant farmers and rural manufacturers in the last century, the latent surplus population is no longer to be found in the British agricultural regions. But it was found and tapped in the post-war period in the peasant agricultural regions of North Africa, the Middle East, Southern Europe, Asia, Africa, the Caribbean and Central America—to name only the most important sites. As capitalism has become a global system of production, so has its sources of labour.

Marx's first category—that of the floating population of young adult male workers—does not exist in its original form. The practice of sacking juvenile workers when they reached an age to be able to command adult wages persisted on a wide scale up to the second world war—especially in the textile and coal industries.[10] But in the post-war period, due to the extension of secondary and further education, the sources of juvenile labour dried up as many individuals now entered the labour market in their late teens or even early twenties. However, in the last ten years, overall lack of demand for labour coupled with employers' reluctance to hire young 'undisciplined' workers has created a significant layer of young adult unemployed throughout the West—male and female. So a 'floating population' still exists—but in a modern form and for different reasons from those described by Marx.

A few clarifications are now in order. The surplus population is not another term for the lumpenproletariat. Marx specifically excluded the lumpenproletariat (which he saw as being largely composed of vagabonds, criminals and prostitutes) from the surplus population in the analysis referred to above. But he tended to use the term both vaguely and perjoratively, and it is this latter use which has remained lodged in many socialists' brains. It had a limited use in nineteenth century Europe in referring to a layer of people who had drifted to the bottom of early industrial society through the destruction of pre-capitalist social formations: 'that passively rotting mass thrown off by the lowest layers of old society' as the *Communist Manifesto* put it.[11] But in modern metropolitan society there is no 'old society', and it is hard enough to find sizeable groups corresponding to the lumpenproletariat of Marx's day, let alone ascribe to them the important political role they assumed as a tool of reaction.

Marx, when writing of the unemployed, used both the term the surplus population and the reserve army of labour. We need to distinguish between them. The reserve army of labour has two essential functions in Marx's analysis of capitalism: to supply the labour power when a branch of production suddenly expands 'without injury to the scale of production in other spheres'; and to regulate wages so that an increase in the reserve army depresses wages, and a decrease raises them. It is this latter function which presents problems. In modern society, with our organised labour movement, there is no such automatic connection between the size of the surplus population and wages, if indeed there ever was. As the example of Britain shows, unemployment could rise fourfold during the seventies without adversely affecting the real wages of the vast majority of those in full-time employment. The term 'reserve army of labour' has an economistic flavour, omitting class consciousness and class organisation from its terms of reference; moreover, the surplus population embraces a wider stratum of the working class than those who are just unemployed and as such is more useful in analysing life in the older working class areas than the concept of the reserve army of labour.

Our understanding of the crisis in the older working class areas starts from an awareness that it is a crisis of political and social relations generated by the uneven development of the capitalist system. Underpinning this crisis has been the build-up and concentration of the surplus population in these areas—a build-up which is continuing in these localities but is also now set to take place elsewhere. This swelling of the surplus population is a product of the contradictions besetting the international economic order; its relative concentration in the older urban areas results from the way in which the repercussions of patterns of development and underdevelopment established during the post-war boom are now being felt during a phase of stagnation. But the expansion of the surplus population and the opening up of breaches between it and the rest of the working class are not only symptoms of the economic crisis, but also major inputs into the political crisis that flows from economic stagnation.

As we have seen, the parliamentary right has already

exploited the division between the surplus population and the more prosperous layers of the working class on the electoral plane. And as we shall be analysing later, the problems of public order arising from the expansion and relative concentration of the surplus population have already played a major role in facilitating an important restructuring of the law-and-order apparatus in Britain. Moreover, the return of mass unemployment brings with it obvious problems for the trade unions, not only because it weakens unity by increasing fear of job loss among the employed, but also because it means that a larger and larger segment of the adult working class lacks both experience of or point of entry into the labour movement. Looking slightly further ahead we will be arguing that, in the struggles that are likely to take place in a Britain caught in an era of relative decline the surplus population itself may play a crucial role.

The political role that the surplus population plays at any particular point in history depends on a large number of factors, including its spatial concentration, its social composition and the consciousness of the various groups that fall within it, its cohesion or lack of it, and its relationship to organisations representing the more prosperous layers of the working class. Not least among the factors impinging on the structure of class relations is, of course, the relative weight of the surplus population within society as a whole. In Britain today we are entering a period during which unemployment has and is rising dramatically as a result both of the objective conditions in the world market and the strategy adopted by the state for restoring the conditions for profitable accumulation of capital. This strategy embraces an attempt to maximise divisions within the working class and an attack on the standard of living of all the groups that fall within our definition of the surplus population.

The rest of this book concentrates on an investigation of the forces determining the expansion of the surplus population, its distribution and its role in contemporary Britain. Chapter 1 begins this process by looking at the climate of depression enveloping the international economic order, which is precipitating the build-up of unemployment in Britain, and relating the period we live in to past phases of modern history in which the surplus population has played an important political role.

1. A Long Phase of Stagnation

You who will emerge from the flood
In which we have gone under
Remember
When you speak of our failings
The dark time too
Which you have escaped
For we went, changing countries oftener than our shoes
Through the wars of the classes, despairing
When there was injustice only, and no rebellion.

From Brecht's 'To Those Born Later'
in *Later Svendborg Poems 1936–38*

The seventies will be remembered as the decade in which unemployment in the industrialised world rose to levels higher than any experienced for forty years, the real value of paper money fell by more than half (by two-thirds in Britain), and capitalism's long post-war boom was officially declared dead. In the last half of the decade in particular, heightening competition between capitalist enterprises and imperialist nations became ever more obvious, as did the failure of the strategies previously employed by Western governments to restore the conditions for profitable expansion. Yet for twenty years after the second world war most people thought that the convulsions which seized the international economic system during the inter-war period had been left behind forever. Economists and technocrats seemed to have unlocked the secrets of economic management; mass unemployment had been eradicated and average living standards in the central capitalist societies seemed to be set on an endless upward trajectory. As industrial production and world trade had multiplied the profits earned by investors remained high and even less successful capitalist economies like the British one underwent a marked expansion.

But by the end of the sixties average company profits in the majority of the main economies were already set on a path of long-term decline. In Britain average profits in industry and commerce had fallen from 7.0 per cent of assets employed between 1960-64 to 4.1 per cent in 1970.[1] In the USA, the post-tax rate of profit of non-financial companies had declined from 8.3 per cent between 1961-65 to 5.3 per cent in 1970.[2] In the following five years this downward trend continued in all the central capitalist states—in Japan, for example, the rate of return for industrial companies fell from a high of 22.7 per cent in 1970 to 9.5 per cent in 1975.[3]

A major factor in this declining profitability was militancy among workers whose bargaining power had been strengthened by the long period of 'full employment'. In 1968-69, for example, there were widespread strikes and large wage rises in many European countries, as well as agitations over social issues which were only defused by increases in state expenditure. In the USA the black struggle and the Vietnam debacle created analogous pressures. This contributed to worldwide inflation, as wages and state spending rose faster than production and capitalists attempted to maintain profitability by increasing prices. In response most governments applied deflationary measures, cutting spending, restricting credit, and precipitating a sharp recession and rise in unemployment during 1970-71. In classic Keynesian fashion reflation was then pursued. But with profitability in manufacturing still low, commodity speculation—rather than new investment and employment growth—was the principal characteristic of the hollow boom that followed.

When the crash came in 1974-75 it was the worst since 1929. Bankruptcies soared, financial panic followed a series of banking failures, markets contracted, over 10 per cent of industrial capacity went out of use and investment fell by 13 per cent. As if in defiance of economic logic, inflation accelerated despite falling demand—peaking at over 20 per cent in Britain and Japan, 19 per cent in Italy, 14 per cent in France and 11 per cent in the USA.[4] The oil price rises enforced by OPEC, although not causing the crisis, exacerbated it—as did the monetary restraint governments pursued in order to dampen inflation and defend their exchange rates. Officially recognised unemployment in the six major capitalist economies rose substantially throughout the seventies and, as Table 1 shows, was at a new peak in autumn 1980.

Between 1976 and 1979 a measure of stability was restored to the international monetary system but economic growth remained sluggish, investment depressed and profits low by comparison with the standards of the long boom. Despite fierce rationalisation

Table 1: Officially Recorded Unemployment in the Main Capitalist States

Gross totals and percentage of economically active unemployed

		1968	1970	1972	1974	1976	1978	Sept./ Oct. 1980
UK	millions	0.58	0.61	0.87	0.61	1.35	1.44	2.06
	%	2.5	2.6	3.8	2.6	5.7	6.1	8.5
West Germany	millions	0.32	0.14	0.24	0.58	1.06	0.87	0.88
	%	1.5	0.7	1.1	2.6	4.6	3.9	3.8
USA	millions	2.81	4.08	4.84	5.07	7.28	6.32	7.83
	%	3.6	4.9	5.6	5.6	7.7	6.2	7.5
France	millions	0.25	0.26	0.38	0.49	0.93	1.17	1.52
	%	—	—	—	—	—	4.7	6.8
Italy*	millions	0.68	0.61	0.69	0.56	0.73	1.45	1.75
	%	3.5	3.2	3.7	2.9	3.7	6.8	7.9
Japan	millions	0.59	0.59	0.73	0.73	1.08	1.26	1.15
	%	1.2	1.2	1.4	1.4	2.0	2.4	2.0
Total	millions	5.23	6.29	7.75	8.04	12.43	12.51	15.19

*a new definition of unemployment was adopted in 1977

Source: International Labour Organisation Yearbooks for relevant years. Last column: Financial Times 'World economic Indicators', 9 November 1980.

severe overcapacity has persisted across major metropolitan industries such as steel, shipbuilding, motor vehicles, heavy engineering and textiles. Apart from major contractions in these and other sectors, which have been declining in relative importance for some time, overcapacity has also become evident in some of the prime 'growth sectors' of the post-war period such as synthetics, petrochemicals and electronic consumer durables. International competition has sharpened into sporadic 'trade wars' and the pressures on governments to protect markets and keep imports out have multiplied. Attempts to revive high growth rates via international co-operation have met with conspicuous failure. The USA's weakening competitive position had already led to the collapse of the international monetary system revolving round the strong dollar by the early seventies—since then it has precluded the USA fulfilling its former role of firing world trade by running a persistent balance of payments deficit.

Calls for all the major states to take expansionary measures in concert were resisted by stronger economies such as Germany and Japan who refused to run the risk of higher domestic inflation. By 1979, with inflation rising and renewed recession on the horizon, the attempt had been abandoned and governments everywhere were engaged in an international interest rate war, credit restraint and expenditure cuts—the exact 'monetarist' opposite of the strategies previously employed to combat recession. The new strategy is being pursued not merely in spite of the effect of higher unemployment, but because of it. For many of those in power now reason that, if long-term growth is to be renewed, profits must be sharply raised over a prolonged period—and to do that the big stick of mass unemployment must be brought to bear on the workforce.

At the time of writing it seems clear that the effects of the 1980-81 international recession will not be as severe as that of 1974-75; but it is also clear that its impact in Britain will be extreme. World industrial output is expected to fall by 0.5 per cent in 1981. In the UK however, the most reliable forecasts indicate that manufacturing output will be 16 per cent below its 1979 level in 1982 and unemployment will rise to 3 million—well over double its 1979 level.[5]

Long waves in capitalism

The recent transition from a period of pronounced expansion to one of relative stagnation is not the first to have occurred in the history of industrial capitalism—for over the last two hundred years there have been a succession of such alternating periods and transitions. As Ernest Mandel has written:

> Economic historians are practically unanimous in distinguishing major expansion in the years 1843-73, pronounced long-term depression in the years 1873-93, a tempestuous increase in economic activity in the years 1893-1913, strongly decelerated if not stagnant and regressive development between the two world wars, and a renewed major increase in growth after the second world war. Only with regard to the . . . alleged alteration of faster growth, 1793-1823, and of slower growth 1824-47, is there any, partially justified doubt.[6]

There has also been broad agreement among political economists about some of the main characteristics of long phases of expansion and stagnation. Among the most obvious general characteristics of the long historical phases of expansion in the capitalist system have been:

(a) high growth rates in world trade and industrial production together with a tendency for booms in economic activity to be protracted, while recessions are brief.

(b) radical extensions of the depth and breadth of industrialisation as dynamic industrial bases have been built up in previously lagging countries (e.g. Germany and the USA at the end of the nineteenth century, Japan in the post-war period) and major new growth industries have come to the fore (e.g. electronics and petrochemicals in the post-war period).

(c) expansion of the dimensions of the capitalist market, either geographically as new countries are incorporated into the capitalist system (e.g. the breaking open of new markets for British manufactured goods in the first half of the nineteenth century, the race between the imperialist powers to divide up the globe in the later decades of the century), or as new areas of life are brought to market (e.g. the growth of the leisure, entertainment and tourism industries since the war).

(d) a tendency for the demand for labour to remain buoyant in the major capitalist states, for further social groups to be incorporated into the workforce and for working class living standards to rise.

(e) rapid increases in the productivity of labour in the central capitalist economies as a result of massive renewal and transformation of the infrastructure employed in the production and distribution of goods and services.

The most obvious general characteristics of the long phases of relative stagnation have been the antitheses of those listed above: slackening growth of world trade and industrial production, declining investment in new means of production, sustained depressions being broken only by brief and often primarily speculative booms, heightening competition between capitalist enterprises, growing tensions between the main capitalist nations, often accompanied by government action to protect national home markets for native capitalists; a tendency for living standards in the major capitalist societies to stagnate or even decline, and for unemployment to remain high as the demand for labour outstrips supply over long periods.

It is when one turns from general characteristics of the long phases of capitalist history to the reasons why they occur, and the relationship between the various phenomena, that the difficulties begin. Among marxists, discussion about the nature of such long phases first became prominent in the twenties, when two of the main contributors to the debate were the Russian economist N. D. Kondratieff and Leon Trotsky.[7] It was a period not unlike today, when it had become clear that formidable contradictions beset the international economic order and that the end of the war, far from ushering in a return to pronounced growth, had in fact marked the beginning of a period characterised by recurrent economic crisis and class conflict in Europe. Following hard on the heels of the Russian revolution, the severity of the crisis of 1920-22—which threw millions out of work—led many socialists and communists to believe that the 'inevitable collapse of capitalism' was at hand.

Kondratieff disagreed with this and claimed that the effect of the 1920-21 crisis had been to weaken rather than intensify the contradictions besetting the international capitalist order. Attempting to put contemporary events into a much longer historical perspective, he introduced the concept of 'long cycles'. He argued that between 1789 and 1896 capitalism had experienced two complete long cycles of roughly fifty years, within each of which an expanding wave had been followed by a declining one. The 1920-21 crisis, he asserted, signposted the end of the expanding wave of the third long cycle and the coming years would be dominated by an undertow of stagnation. This did not mean, however, that the end of the capitalist system was imminent.

In the following years Kondratieff outlined the mechanism through which he saw these cycles operating. In doing so he linked his theory of long cycles tightly to Marx's analysis of the short-term seven to ten year business cycle:

> Marx asserted that the material basis of crises, or average cycles, repeating themselves each decade, is the material wearing out, replacement and expansion of the mass of means of production in the form of machines lasting an average of ten years . . . it can be suggested that the material basis of long cycles is the wearing out, replacement and expansion of fixed capital goods which require a long period of time and enormous expenditures to produce.[8]

The rising wave of a long cycle, Kondratieff held, presupposed a long period of saving in excess of investment in new means of production and the gathering of these funds into the hands of potential investors, confronted with sufficiently profitable opportunities to make massive investments in new generations of machines, buildings, transport systems etc. At this point the new investment wave would occur and its transforming effects would 'ultimately contribute to social and political instability; and this fact, together with a gradual depletion of loanable funds, would cause the interest rate to rise. Investment would then be curtailed, a declining wave would ensue, and 'the incentive to discover cost cutting innovations would be restored'.[9]

Kondratieff also argued that phenomena such as political instability, revolutions, wars, technological innovation and the incorporation of new countries into the world market were all specifically associated with different phases of the long cycle mechanism.

Throughout the 1920s up to 1930—when the Russian economist disappeared in a Stalinist purge—Trotsky was engaged in a dispute with Kondratieff. There were, however, basic points of agreement between them. Thus Trotsky—addressing the Third Congress of the Communist International in 1921—affirmed his belief that the great economic crisis of the time did not herald the end of capitalism and that an upswing would occur in the immediate future—though this would be short and would not rule out the possibility of socialist revolution in Europe. He went on to say—with remarkable foresight—that if, after two or three decades, the struggle for socialism was to suffer a lasting setback (as it would do with fascism and war) then there would be the possibility of renewed long-term expansion within the capitalist framework. Trotsky also agreed with Kondratieff's periodisation of economic history—but he strongly rejected the economist's analysis that the transition between epochs of expansion and stagnation was determined by the same 'internal dynamic of capitalist forces' which governs the business cycle. The character of such long phases, Trotsky wrote:

> is determined not by the internal play of capitalist forces, but by the external conditions in which capitalist development occurs. The absorption by capitalism of new countries and continents, the discovery of new natural resources, and, in addition, significant factors of a 'superstructural order' such as wars and revolutions, determine the character and alteration of expansive stagnating or declining epochs in capitalist development.[10]

In modern terms this amounts to a rejection of Kondratieff's 'economism' and an affirmation that it is social and political relations which ultimately determine whether capitalism collapses or survives, and not its own mysterious laws.

The most important recent contribution to the debate is

undoubtedly contained in Ernest Mandel's *Late Capitalism*. Central to this very rich work is Mandel's own exposition of the theory of long waves, within which the rate of profit is seen as the key regulator. As Bob Rowthorne wrote in his 1976 review of the book:

> In essence Mandel's basic theory is rather simple. Accumulation depends on the rate of profit, and anything which raises the latter stimulates accumulation. The expansionary phase of a long wave occurs when the rate of profit is lifted radically upwards by what he calls 'triggering factors' . . . It draws to a close when the effect of these triggering factors begins to wear off, as their potential is exhausted and the rate of profit begins to fall . . . A new expansionary phase occurs when the rate of profit is once again lifted radically upwards by some new combination of factors. Thus capitalism develops in a series of spurts, each initiated by an external shock, whose effect is gradually dissipated by the process of accumulation itself.[11]

Among the 'triggering factors' Mandel lists are: a radical fall in the cost of raw materials; a sudden expansion of the world market or the opening up of new fields for the profitable investment of capital; a sudden increase in the rate of surplus value due to a 'radical defeat or atomisation of the working class'; a sudden fall in the cost of plant and machinery; and the perfection of new systems of transport and distribution. He argues that when sufficiently strong combinations of such factors have had the effect of bringing about a long-run rise in the rate of profit earned by capitalists, capital which has laid idle during the previous long phase of stagnation is once again invested and a 'fundamental renewal of productive technology' occurs. Each of the last three long expansionary phases in capitalist history, Mandel holds, have been accompanied by distinct 'technological revolutions' which have radically raised the productivity of labour in the central capitalist economies. Specifically, he sees these technological revolutions as having revolved around the machine production of steam driven engines and their generalisation throughout the various branches of manufacturing and transport during the expansionary phase beginning about 1848, the machine production and widening application of electric and combustion engines beginning in the nineties of the last century, and the machine production and generalisation of electronic and nuclear powered apparatuses since the nineteen forties.

A certain unreal symmetry accompanies some of Mandel's generalisations about the various epochs of capitalist development, and other strands of his theory—the precise nature and centrality of the 'third technological revolution' he identifies, for example—would seem to be open to criticism on empirical grounds. Nevertheless his general approach to capitalist development is very useful in providing:

> a conceptual framework within which to consider the effect of a wide variety of technological, economic and political factors; yet at the same time, it maintains a close connection with classical marxism by focusing on the internal dynamics of the long wave itself and emphasising the inherent tendency of accumulation to undermine the foundations of its own success.[11]

By focusing on the rate of profit as crucial, and stressing the wide variety of factors that can impinge on it, he shortcircuits the dispute about whether capitalism's 'internal dynamics' or 'external conditions' are determining. This approach also enables him to locate successive long cycles within a continuum without losing sight of the historically specific nature of the various phases of capitalist development and the turning points between them.

Such an analysis of how the conditions for renewed long-term expansion have been created during previous long phases of stagnation is highly relevant precisely because we have entered a comparable phase within the last ten years. From a capitalist point of view, the barriers to continued accumulation that became apparent during the mid-seventies have not been overcome. Imperialist domination of the world market has been threatened by a series of defeats. Rising energy and raw material costs remain a major constraint on accumulation in the metropolitan states and, while no significant anti-capitalist offensive has developed there, the metropolitan working class remains highly organised. Nowhere has it yet suffered a 'radical defeat or atomisation' capable of contributing to a long-run rise in the rate of profit. In short, the question of whether and how the capitalist class can secure the conditions for profitable expansion remains unanswered. It seems that major battles to decide whether growth is resumed according to capitalist or socialist priorities lie ahead.

In such a situation socialist strategy needs to be informed by historical experience—but we have to be able to draw lessons relevant to today from previous long phases of stagnation without making misleading or mechanical historical comparisons. To this end the next section looks back to the end of the nineteenth century and the inter-war period, outlining the dominant factors that served then to bring about a long-run rise in the rate of profit.

In introducing this historical perspective, prior to drawing the conclusions we believe are relevant to Britain today, we want to stress two points. First, that while capitalist recovery has been brought about by a different combination of factors in each period, mass suffering and destruction on a truly vile scale has been a necessary part of the process every time. The second point is that while the last long phase of stagnation manifested itself on a world scale, it had very different repercussions domestically depending on the relative competitive strength of the different national economies in the international order. Where these repercussions were at their most severe, divisions within the working class were crucial to the outcome of the struggle that followed.

The great depression

By the beginning of the 1870s European industrialisation—which had really taken off after 1848—had reached an initial ceiling. The technological transformation that had begun with the application of steam power in the mines had spread not only through heavy industry and the consumer goods branches but also to transport, both on land and at sea. The greater scope of industrialisation was accompanied by its greater spread—Britain was no longer the clear leader but was now one of a number of great industrial powers. The growth of capitalist industry in Europe led to increasing competition, and selling in foreign markets became more difficult as tariff barriers were erected to secure national markets for native entrepreneurs. This heightened competition became particularly obvious when a trade depression, beginning in 1873, eliminated many smaller enterprises. At the same time other long-term trends were cutting into the profit margins of capital in general.

The first wave of industrialisation, in progressively destroying the old craft organisation of production, had created labour reserves of immense size as hundreds of thousands of workers migrated to the new centres of industry. There, the competition for work served to both depress wages and hamper labour organisation. But from the mid-century onwards a steady migration overseas, especially to North America, facilitated the growth of trade unionism in Western Europe—and proletarian organisation was reflected in a steady rise in real wages.[13] Another trend which was cutting into the profit margins of industrial capital was the rising cost of many raw materials. As competition for supplies between the cost of finishing industries was accompanied by unsatisfied demand the attendant rise in prices had served to narrow the gap between producing a given article and what it fetched on the market. Thus by the 1870s the general struggle between capitals not only involved exacerbated competition for markets but for secure sources of cheap raw materials as well. A period of stagnation followed in which falling profits combined with the emergence of an excess of capital which could no longer be profitably invested where it had accumulated.

Prior to this period the capital accumulated by the owners of industry remained relatively immobile—it was mainly invested in their own enterprises or in new industrial activities in the same national market. Foreign investment played a small part in economic activity and was almost exclusively British in origin. Furthermore exported British capital went mainly to Europe and North America in the form of loans designed to finance railway building and secure a market for the products of heavy industry. From the 1870s onwards, however, this pattern changed radically as the export of goods alone gave way to the export of capital, and trading expeditions gave way to annexation and colonisation of other continents. Previously, while the long upsurge of internal industrialisation had guaranteed high profits, the captains of industry had been hungry for resources and had consistently attacked all forms of state expenditure. Now they supported it—so long as it was directed towards the capture of new fields for the profitable investment of capital.

The age of imperialist expansion stretched from 1875 to 1914—it was the period in which the world market was truly fashioned into a unity of antagonistic parts. For investors, the attraction of the colonial and semi-colonial world lay in the possibility of mobilising and disciplining vast armies of cheap labour in such a way that extraordinary profits could be earned over long historical periods. Capital invested in the plantations and mines had been transferred from countries in which wages were tending to rise to ones in which brutal measures were used to produce conditions of super exploitation, even worse than those that had existed in Europe at the onset of the industrial revolution.

The capital invested there had also been transferred from industrial sectors in which the mass of machinery was rising relative to the amount of living labour it could bring into play, thus forcing down the rate of profit. It moved into a type of production where the same quantity of capital could bring a very much larger amount of human labour into action and so increase its rate of profit. In addition, at a time when competition in Europe was intensifying, it was limited in the colonial world by virtue of the fact that the production of this or that commodity was effectively monopolised by a very small number of large trusts—the colonial venture from the outset being too large for small capital. All these factors allowed capital invested in the colonies to realise surplus profits in both the expansionary phase of imperialism and inter-war period that followed—it was quite common for the yield of overseas investment to fluctuate between 30 per cent and 20 per cent per annum whilst industrial capital in the metropolis earned between 7 per cent and 15 per cent.[14]

Imperialism and the world division of labour ushered in by capital export also worked to the general advantage of the capitalist class in Western Europe. By the beginning of the 1890s capital had effectively spread over a wider field of action, so reducing competition and effecting a slight enlargement of the market for metropolitan goods. Increased production of agricultural and mineral raw materials also effected a reversal of the previous trend for their relative prices to rise. In this way imperialist expansion and capital export provided an exit from the impasse that underlay the first clearly defined long phase of relative stagnation in the history of industrial capitalism. Together they played a crucial role in making possible a further upsurge of growth prior to 1914.

In the last quarter of the nineteenth century it was the brutal exploitation of the peoples of Africa, Asia and Latin America that dragged the international capitalist system out of crisis. Heightened competition between capitalist enterprises, between the needs of metropolitan capital and labour, and between the industrialised nations, was in a sense displaced into the race to capture colonies. But as the partition of different continents was completed, small conflicts between the participants became sharper. The sharing out process gave way to a struggle between the major powers for a redistribution of the spoils, culminating in the sudden death of millions in the first world war, a conflict which itself ushered in the ensuing long phase of relative stagnation.

The inter-war period

The outbreak of the first world war had disrupted the previous patterns of world trade, but during its course the European conflict itself provided a massive market for the products of major industries—ensuring that in general the owners of industrial capital continued to reap fat profits. Once the short post-war boom had passed, however, it became clear that there could be no simple return to the pre-war status quo or levels of growth. On the one hand much of the European market was impoverished, while on the other the United States had emerged from the conflict with its industrial power greatly enhanced. Not only had its internal market expanded, but US capital had also captured a significant proportion of Europe's old export markets—particularly in South America. In the ensuing two decades competition for markets was to remain intense, tariff barriers were to proliferate and as a result the average growth in world trade—which had increased in volume by 3.7 per cent annually between 1891 and 1913—only averaged 0.4 per cent between 1913 and 1937.[15]

With the world market fractured and severe overcapacity facing core industries (such as coal, steel, shipbuilding and heavy engineering in Europe in particular), the capitalist class in general was to experience severe difficulty in maintaining the profitability of existing investment. In addition, during the following decades lack of opportunities for profitable investment of accumulated capital served to ensure that real economic growth remained sporadic. Even in the United States—the home of new industries such as motor car and consumer durable manufacture—it fell from a pre-first world war annual average of 5.9 per cent to an inter-war average of 2 per cent.[16] Mass unemployment, while varying in extent from nation to nation, was consequently a feature of every central capitalist economy.

In such a situation of stagnation, every national capitalist class had to seek to restore profits at the expense of the working class. However, the severity of the crisis affected nations unevenly, biting harder in some countries than in others. A brief comparison between Britain and Germany illustrates the political consequences of this unevenness.

By the turn of the century Britain had already entered on the long road of relative industrial decline, with profits from abroad being used to shore up a less productive manufacturing base. Despite the enforced sale of foreign assets during the war and loss of past dominance in the realm of world finance to the United States, the British Empire was still the largest in the world—both in terms of population and land mass. After the war, class struggle on the terrain of declining industries led to the General Strike—but once this had been defeated no serious threat to the rule of capital emerged. Cheap food supplies from the colonies cushioned the fall in real wages and the full effects of 10 per cent unemployment. The Empire also provided a protected market for the products of the new consumer goods industries that were the major focus of real economic growth in Britain during the thirties.

The combined effects of Britain's position within the world market, and the relatively early defeat of the working class, ensured that industrial restructuring on capital's terms (along with the restoration of profitability) took place within the framework of parliamentary democracy. When mass unemployment began to rise sharply again in 1929-30, the working class had already suffered the historic defeat of the General Strike, which had strengthened the reformist leadership of the labour movement and weakened the influence of the Communist Party within the working class. Despite this, the British CP was able to successfully organise the unemployed who were mainly concentrated in the old industrial regions. This organisation—in the form of the National Unemployed Workers Movement—was a major factor ensuring that fascism never gained ground in the crisis-ridden regions.

In contrast to Britain, Germany had lost the battle for redistribution of markets and colonies and seen its former possessions fall under the 'protection' of other national capitals. The gathering inter-war crisis was all the more intense in Germany, for not only had markets and colonies been lost, but war reparations subsequently had to be made to the victorious allies. The pressure on the German capitalist class was amplified by the presence of the German Communist Party, which, despite the disastrous twists and turns of Comintern policy, remained Europe's strongest communist party outside Russia up until Hitler's accession to power. In every respect, the pressures on the capitalist class were greater in Germany than in Britain, the stakes higher, and the results of confrontation and defeat far more terrible. The depth of the contradictions besetting the capitalist system in inter-war Germany ensured that their resolution within that system could not be found within the confines of parliamentary democracy. That required fascism—which brought about startlingly successful results for the capitalist class: the average hourly wage fell from an index figure of 129.5 in 1929 to 108.6 in 1939, while the mass of profit increased by some 30 per cent in the same period.[17] Thus Hitler's victory and the subsequent destruction of the German labour movement allowed German capital to substitute an internal source of extraordinary profits for its lost external source. And at the same time it created the social conditions for a resurgent German imperialism which challenged the division of the world market laid down at the end of the first world war. The triumph of fascism in Italy, the defeat of the General Strike in 1926, the crash of 1929, the seizure of power by Hitler and Franco all arose from, or led to, crisis situations that were resolved in favour of the particular ruling class in the countries involved. As such they allowed the capitalist class to begin to impose, on a national scale, its own solution to the economic crisis enveloping the international system at that time—by restoring profitability at the expense of the working class.

The profitability of existing investments was gradually restored throughout significant sections of the metropolitan economy. But, in the context of a world market fractured by protectionist barriers, capital that had lain idle during the depression was only very slowly drawn back into production. Overcapacity still existed in key industrial sectors such as coal, iron, steel and shipbuilding; while the extension of production that could be achieved in the growth industries of the time (such as cars and electrical consumer goods) was sharply limited by the narrowness of the potential market. In such conditions it took rearmament and the massive extension of the market achieved by a war-economy to take up the slack throughout the metropolitan countries and draw surplus capital into a vortex of rising industrial production. The defeats of the working class made possible a temporary resolution to the crisis on capitalist terms within the confines of the nation state. They did not in themselves resolve the heightened international capitalist competition that characterised the inter-war period—but they were an essential prerequisite for working class participation in the bloody and violent conflict from which the necessary conditions for the post-war boom emerged.

World war redistributes spheres of influence, ruins sections of the bourgeoisie and forces the temporary withdrawal of others from the field—in doing so, it serves a function by dampening for a time the acute competition that has preceded it. Thus by 1946 Germany, Italy and Japan had been defeated and much of their industrial infrastructure had been destroyed or put out of action. The war appeared to mark the triumph of American imperialism. But world war has proved to be double-edged for the capitalist class in stoking the fires of revolt and revolution. So in 1946, as in 1918, the geographical extent of the capitalist world market had once again been narrowed and the political complexion of the

41

post-war settlement hung in the balance. In Japan the process of 'democratising' the militarist state was leading to a flowering of left-wing thought and organisation as banned socialist and communist groups came out of hiding. In China civil war raged between communists and nationalists, in India the anti-colonialist movement was gaining ground, the Yugoslav resistance army had not only liberated the country from fascism but overthrown the old social order. Eastern Europe was occupied by the victorious Red Army and a form of social revolution had been initiated. In Italy, France and Greece the communist-led resistance movements had emerged from the conflict in control of large areas of both countries. In Britain working class response to the end of the war, although safely channelled into the confines of social democracy, had led to the election of the first Labour government with a parliamentary majority. In the United States itself a powerful strike wave produced massive wage rises.

In the following years order was brought into this chaos via a two-pronged strategy spearheaded by the American state. The first part of the strategy involved an anti-communist offensive on a world scale, designed to create the necessary political conditions for growth within a capitalist framework. Armed intervention against communist partisans was used in countries as widely separated as Greece and Indo-China. In Japan 'democratisation' was abandoned in favour of 'the reverse course': the power of the old ruling groups was now left intact, civil liberties were curtailed and a 'red purge' was initiated. In France and Italy the communist parties, committed to a parliamentary strategy, were now unceremoniously expelled from the governments of national reconstruction. In Germany a similar 'reverse course' was applied by the Allies: building an anti-communist state now took precedence over limiting the power of those who had been part of the Nazi régime. As in Japan, fresh obstacles to the rebirth of an independent labour movement now became enshrined in the constitution imposed by the Allied powers. In the United States two years of post-war industrial militancy were brought to an end with the imposition of the anti-strike Taft-Hartley Act. At the same time the launching of an ideological offensive prepared the ground for the incorporation of the trade union bureaucracy into the Cold War strategy. McCarthyism effectively weeded out militants from industry, destroyed the communist party and suppressed political dissent.

The second prong of this strategy involved putting the finishing touches to a new international economic order, which revolved around the ability of US capitalism to underwrite the renewal of economic growth in Western Europe and the Far East. In its formal aspects this new international order was founded in 1944 at Bretton Woods, where agreements reached between the Allies foreshadowed the creation of the International Monetary Fund, the International Bank for Reconstruction and Development and the General Agreement on Tariffs and Trades. The aim of these agreements was to create a mechanism whereby world demand could be maintained at a high level and a framework for a liberalisation of trade and capital movement which would prevent a return to the inter-war fragmentation of the world market. They thus reflected, at an international level, a new attitude on the part of the bourgeoisie to state intervention in the economy, an attitude that stemmed directly from the experience of the thirties.

From the standpoint of the eighties we can see that the success of the system depended on the pre-eminence of the United States' economy and on its ability to finance the expansion of world trade by running a persistent deficit on its balance of payments—once this pre-eminence had been eroded, increasing strains on the international monetary system revolving round a strong dollar became inevitable. We can also see that domestic demand management, and the whole range of anti-cyclical (or anti-crisis) state interventions, tended to prolong growth in the central capitalist economies at the cost of institutionalising inflation.

Britain today

Since the upswing of capitalist industrialisation at the end of the eighteenth century, economic activity has moved forward through distinct long phases, dominated in turn either by strongly expansionary tendencies or an underflow of stagnation. During these latter periods the contradictions inherent in a system based on the exploitation of labour by capital have broken surface with major implications not only for economic activity, but also for social and political life at many levels.

In the thirties and forties fascism, world war and further political defeats for the working class played a crucial role in laying the foundations of the long boom. In the eighties and nineties an equally radical shift in the international balance of class forces may well be required before growth can be resumed in the central capitalist states. But tomorrow's conflicts will not be mere re-runs of yesterday's. They cannot fail but reflect the major shifts that have occurred in the relative strengths of the dominant economies, the enormously expanded dimensions of the 'socialist' bloc and the continuing struggles of third world peoples to wrest control of their own countries from outside exploitation. Similarly, the internal conflicts which are already arising in the central capitalist states issue from the way in which the capitalist economy has been restructured during the post-war period, the role of the modern state and the way in which the working class has been recomposed.

Nevertheless two general points drawn from observation of the last two long phases of stagnation are particularly relevant to us in Britain today. The first is that where the national repercussions of international stagnation are at their most severe, securing a major radical increase in the rate of exploitation of large sections of the working class becomes an imperative for capital. The UK is no longer in such a privileged position within the world order that the effects of stagnation are muted by comparison with other capitalist nations. On the contrary, it is in an analogously weak position to that of Germany and Italy during the twenties. Deindustrialisation has gathered pace and the overall expansion of the world market no longer serves to mitigate the effects of declining competitiveness. And there can be little doubt that a major factor in the UK's relative decline has been the strength of an organised working class which, as Mandel has written, was:

> the only major proletariat in the world which suffered no serious defeat for thirty years from 1936 to 1966—an experience which profoundly modified the relationship of class forces in England. Thus Britain became the only imperialist power which was unable to increase the rate of exploitation of its working class significantly during or after the second world war . . . from a capitalist point of view, the result was evident: an erosion of the rate of profit, and a much slower rate of economic growth and accumulation than in the other imperialist countries.[18]

Recent history clearly shows the need for British capital, acting through the state, to take on the organised working class. Since the late sixties every administration has been preoccupied not only with holding down wages, but also with the problem of 'overmanning', the obstructiveness of shop-floor organisation and the need to increase productivity in industry. Today the Thatcher government is approaching the task of increasing the rate of exploitation in a muscular fashion—but it is by no means clear that the ruling class will be able to succeed in creating the conditions for renewed growth within the framework of parliamentary democracy and traditional democratic freedoms. Indeed, the 1980 Brookings Institute report on the UK economy—which analysed Britain's decline in terms of the problem of productivity—concluded that, because 'the problem originates deep within the social system, one needs an optimistic disposition to suppose that a democratic political system can eliminate that problem.'[19]

Our second point concerns the process of class conflict that occurs in those societies where the long wave of stagnation has a particularly strong impact—and the role of those that have no secure place in those societies because they have become marginalised by the dominant trends of capitalist development. If we look back to Germany and Italy between the wars, we can see that the impact of the crisis was such that it was impossible for it to be resolved without there first having been a major shift in the balance of class forces. We can also see that while the backing of the owners of heavy industry was crucial in bringing fascism to power, the depressed middle classes (robbed of their former privileges by monopolisation and inflation) and the unemployed (swollen in number by the depth of the crisis) provided fascism with, in turn, both a mass base and its storm troopers. The alienation of both groups from the organised working class was of crucial strategic importance as the struggle unfolded.[20]

Fascism as it evolved in the inter-war period will not reoccur in Britain, or any other metropolitan country, because the particular social and political order it emerged from has long since passed. But it is nonetheless clear that the relationship of the 'surplus population' to the organisations of the working class has once again become one of critical strategic importance. As we will argue in Chapter 6, it has already had a bearing on the shift to 'the strong state' in Britain. The relationship between the 'surplus population' and the organised working class today springs from the way that the working class has been recomposed throughout the post-war period and the differential impact the crisis is having on different groups in the population. This process is examined in the next chapter.

2. The Changing Shape of the Working Class

The socialist movement in Europe has experienced great difficulty in coming to terms with the way that the transformation wrought in the course of the post-war boom has recomposed the working class. Bruising battles have often broken out as different groups on the young revolutionary wing of the movement have castigated their rivals for failing to win an authentic working class membership or following. Frequently, those who engage in these dogfights hold a mirror to themselves, framed in the twenties, and swirling with images of cloth-capped miners and engineers confronting not only the capitalist class, but also a uniformly hostile middle class and intelligentsia. All too often the real working class is seen as male, manual and white. Such an attitude uneasily combines a militant determination to gain influence among the traditional sectors of the working class and a nostalgic conservatism about the nature of the modern proletariat. It ignores the way that the expansion of the capitalist market has led to new groups being drawn directly into waged labour, destroyed old skills and integrated mental labour into the processes of production. It cherishes the gulf between intellectuals and workers, and between men and women, at a time when the evolution of the capitalist mode of production is laying the objective basis for overcoming these divides.

In fact it is in the urban core that the greatest concentrations of female and black labour are to be found and the workforce as a whole corresponds least to the male, manual and white stereotype. Here too the capitalist economy itself—with its proliferation of service sector activities at street level and its stark office buildings puncturing the skyline—now approximates least to the inherited images of works, mill and mine.

Harry Braverman's book *Labour and Monopoly Capital* has played a pioneering role in developing an understanding of the way in which the working class has been recomposed during the post-war period. Central to Braverman's study is an analysis of the evolution of labour processes within modern capitalist society—the way in which labour has been shifted between

46

different branches of the economy on the one hand, and the way in which the nature of work has altered within different branches on the other. Adopting Marx's terminology Braverman makes a distinction between these two phenomena, referring to the dynamic process whereby labour has been reallocated to different branches (i.e. agriculture, mining, manufacturing, the personal, state and financial service sectors etc.) as the changing *social division of labour*, and to the way in which the labour process has been transformed within different branches as the changing *detailed (or technical) division of labour*. In this chapter we shall examine the recomposition of the working class in the central capitalist states, and the formation of the surplus population in the wave of stagnation, by way of these categories. We will be arguing, first, that because of the particular stance of US and UK capital during the post-war period, and the history of these two countries' insertion into the world market, certain tendencies in the changing social division of labour have registered earlier in these two societies than elsewhere. Secondly, we will show that due to the particular way these economies tapped new reserves of labour during the long boom, the social and political composition of the surplus population is distinct. The combination of these two factors is the underlying cause of the political impact the surplus population has made in Britain and the US since the mid-sixties.

The social division of labour

Unlike the detailed division of labour, the social division of labour predates capitalism and made its appearance as soon as specialised groups of workers had been assigned to different branches of production—fishing as opposed to farming, craft manufacture as opposed to cultivation, for example. During the upsweep of industrialisation and on into the twentieth century, the social division of labour in the central capitalist economies changed dramatically as the proportion of the working population engaged in agriculture fell. This movement was reinforced by the formation of a world market within which industrial production became concentrated and expanded in the imperialist nations, while the path of 'development' in the colonial world was subjugated to the needs of the imperialist nations for cheap agricultural and mineral raw materials. During the post-war period the proportion of the workforce assigned to agriculture has continued to fall in the imperialist nations. Thus in Japan and France, the percentage of

47

all workers employed on the land fell from 46.7 per cent and 36 per cent respectively in 1950 to 17.7 per cent and 14 per cent in 1970.[1]

But as the post-war period has progressed the shift from agriculture to industry in the metropolitan states has given way to a second tendency in the changing social division of labour. The proportion of the working class employed in the manufacturing sector has risen more slowly, levelled off and begun to fall—while at the same time the proportion employed in the state, personal and financial service sectors has continued to rise.

These trends in the social division of labour within the major capitalist societies are the product of post-war expansion on the one hand, and of the specific nature of the wave of technological transformation on the other. The long boom saw a vast increase in the volume and range of the manufactured goods produced in these countries, and consequently there was an absolute increase in the number of manufacturing sector workers in all these states. However, as automation spread and production was concentrated into high productivity units, soaring output did not require a proportionately increased workforce. The new production technologies in manufacturing and mechanisation of agriculture set free a pool of labour which was absorbed by sectors opened up by the lateral expansion of the capitalist market: the burgeoning personal, financial and state services.

Relatively untouched by electronic information technology these sectors remained labour intensive and also recruited heavily amongst migrant, immigrant and married women workers entering the labour market for the first time. Thus in all the major economies there was a significant increase in the proportion of the workforce engaged in the various branches of the service sector. This trend is illustrated by the OECD labour force statistics which show that all the main economies registered a six point jump in service work as a percentage of total employment between 1957 and 1968. In that year service work, including the financial services, accounted for between 40 per cent and 61 per cent of all jobs in each of the main OECD countries, excepting Canada and Italy.[2]

The impact of these broad trends, operating throughout the metropolitan world during the long boom, was markedly different for each major capitalist economy. As far as manufacturing employment is concerned, it is possible to arrange the major economies in a spectrum of development. At one end of the spectrum stand West Germany and Japan, industrial giants who

48

have come to account for ever greater shares of world trade and industrial production as the post-war period has progressed. As they did so Japan's industrial workforce grew from 15.5 per cent of the total in 1950 to 22.5 per cent in 1970, while Germany's increased from 30.9 per cent to 38.9 per cent over the same period.[3] Other European economies occupy the middle ground—thus while Japan's manufacturing workforce increased by 4.5 million between 1957 and 1968 and Italy's grew by half a million, France's only grew by 281,000, Belgium's by 11,000 and Holland's by 87,000.[4] Britain and the United States stand at the other end of the spectrum—with their shares of world trade and industrial production having been cut, and their manufacturing workforce or classical industrial proletariat declining as a proportion of the whole class. In the USA the proportion of the workforce engaged in manufacturing fell from 26.8 per cent in 1950 to 22.4 per cent in 1976, while the fall in Britain was from 37.3 per cent in 1951 to 32.6 per cent in 1971. Between 1966 and 1976 UK manufacturing employment fell from 8.6m to 7.2m. With the entry into the long wave of stagnation, this trend in the social division of labour has become generalised and the proportion of the class engaged in manufacturing is remaining static or declining in all the major capitalist states. It should be noted that the first signs of this trend originated during the long boom itself both in Britain and the USA.

This uneven development of the social division of labour in the central capitalist states stems from the different stances that the various national groupings of capital adopted vis-à-vis their home states and the world market in the last thirty-five years. Britain emerged from the second world war as an imperial power on the wane—the USA as an imperialist power at the zenith of its influence. We argued in the last chapter that, in Britain's case, the balance of class forces has evolved, since the early defeat of the General Strike, in a disadvantageous way to capital accumulation in Britain itself. In addition, in both countries the survival of worldwide interests accompanied the traditions and habits of overseas investment and throughout the long boom both these economies were to be far more thoroughly dominated by finance capital and large transnational companies than were the other major capitalist economies.

In the fifties, the US was busy shoring up the post-war settlement throughout the West, while the British Empire and its sterling area was still largely intact. In this situation a significant fraction of big capital continued to seek out opportunities for super-exploitation of cheap labour and resources in less developed countries—but at the same time US companies began to invest heavily in European markets, while UK capital continued to flow in the direction of the relatively developed old Commonwealth countries, (South Africa, Canada, New Zealand, Australia). In the sixties, following the US lead, UK capital increasingly turned its attention to Europe and the States itself. As a result of these trends the capitalist class in Britain and America had moved into a position whereby they held 75 per cent of the world stock of direct company investment abroad in 1968.[5] At this time US company production abroad was running at more than three times the level of US exports, while UK company production from overseas plants was double UK exports. Three years later, in 1971, UK investment in manufacturing abroad was estimated to total $10.25 billion (of which 81 per cent was in the developed OECD countries), US investment abroad was $35.6 billion (83 per cent in the industrialised world). By way of comparison, German investment abroad—although rising fast—was only $4.6 billion and Japanese investment in overseas manufacturing was well below $1 billion.[6] US investment in manufacturing abroad had in fact risen from 12 per cent of investment in plant and equipment at home in 1957-61 to 21.2 per cent in 1967-70.[7]

Turning to the figures for overseas direct investment (including reinvested earnings) as a percentage of gross domestic product, Britain emerges as by far and away the leader of overseas investors. Between 1968 and 1978 this flow averaged 1.4 per cent of GDP as opposed to 0.7 per cent for the USA, 0.3 per cent for Japan and 0.5 per cent for Germany.[8]

As one would expect such high rates of investment export— unmatched by equal investment import—have been associated with a relative decline of the manufacturing base of these two economies. The US share of the capitalist world's industrial output fell from an all time high of 52 per cent in 1953 to 40.5 per cent in 1970—over the same period the UK share fell from 10 per cent to 5 per cent.[9] (See also Table 2.)

A similar trend emerges in annual average productivity growth in manufacturing from 1960 to 1978 which shows Japanese and German enterprises far outstripping their US and UK counterparts.

It is worth remembering that these figures do not measure the performance of the top US and UK companies which, by virtue of their transnational operations have continued to prosper— exploiting differences in wages, unionisation levels, land prices,

Table 2: Percentage share of exports from central capitalist economies*

	1950	1960	1970	1977
UK	25.5	16.5	10.8	9.3
France	9.9	9.6	8.7	9.9
Germany	7.3	19.3	19.8	20.8
Japan	3.4	6.9	11.7	15.4
USA	27.3	21.6	18.5	15.9

Source: Table 10.5 in 'De-industrialisation—a background paper' Brown & Sherriff in *De-industrialisation* edited by Frank T. Blackaby, London, Heinemann 1979.

*Listed countries plus Canada, Sweden, Switzerland, Benelux countries and Italy.

etc.—while the manufacturing base of their respective home states has continued to weaken.

The forces shaping the expansion of the Japanese and German economies were quite different to those at work in the USA and the UK. The destruction of the German and Japanese labour movements under fascism, the reimposition of authoritarian rule after 'liberation' and the pump-priming effects of influxes of triumphant US capital in the early post-war years created an exceptionally favourable climate for internal investment. Authoritarian rule in West Germany and the presence of a huge industrial reserve army, swollen by millions of refugees, insured that real wages did not reach their (already depressed) 1938 levels until 1956.[10] At the same time, the destruction of foreign assets and the loss of newly-won colonial possessions effectively retarded transnational expansion from both countries, while the state—shorn of its world role—turned directly to the task of reconstructing the national economy.

In Japan, 'the government was the sole source of capital in the immediate post-war period and the administrators were in control of funds to business and industry.'[11] Subsequently, and to this day, the leaders of the great Japanese monopolies have continued to work very closely with the top government officials and the state has continued to play a prominent role in planning the Japanese export offensive, as well as underwriting loans from financial institutions to the major companies. By doing this the state 'not only makes possible the financing of growth through debt—it also ensures for itself a central role in determining the pace and direction of that growth.'[12]

The German state acted along similarly interventionist lines in the immediate post-war period when, as Landes notes, it:

> disposed of billions of dollars . . . [and] . . . to distribute these to worthy recipients it established the KW, a bank of banks, that sifted out from the recommendations of the private financial institutions those that fitted the national programme. The amounts furnished in this way constituted an important fraction of the 'free funds' available for industrial investment; thus from 1948 to 1953, the KW issued loans totalling 5.5 billion DM, as against 7 billion in new issues of stocks and bonds.[13]

The German state maintained a general ban on foreign investment up to 1952, and after it was relaxed continued to offer substantial subsidies to companies investing at home. Similarly, the Japanese state maintained strict controls on capital export up until the seventies.

By contrast the US state has never tried stringently to check capital export or directed the path of industrial growth in the way that the German and Japanese state apparatuses have. In Britain attempts to promote industrial restructuring in line with the need for international competitiveness have always stopped well short of rigorously controlling capital export.

Over the last decade the pattern of overseas investments has changed as transnational companies have stepped up their efforts to cut labour costs by siting labour-intensive production in low wage countries which are 'safe' for investments. Another significant development has been the entry of Japanese and German capital into the capital export game in a bigger way than ever before. This has been a spur to the relative industrialisation of such countries as South Korea, whose industrialisation, financed largely through Japanese capital, has begun to affect employment levels in Japan, not only in the labour intensive 'twilight sector' but also in more modern sectors like steel and shipbuilding. As this has happened so the proportion of Japan's workforce has ceased its staggering growth and actually declined; while South Korea's manufacturing workforce has increased from 18.4 per cent of the total to 25 per cent between 1971 and 1975. Similar increases were registered in Taiwan, Brazil, Singapore and Iran—all nations where capital flowed in under the protection of repressive regimes.

It seems clear therefore that the relative industrialisation of a number of previously underdeveloped countries and the effects of the crisis are reinforcing the trend for the proportion of the workforce engaged in manufacturing to stagnate and fall throughout the West. As the 1980-81 recession severely grips the US and UK economies, the relative decline of these countries, manufacturing bases appears to be continuing, leading to a greater degree of deindustrialisation than elsewhere in the West.

Up to this point we have stressed the national unevenness in the evolution of the social division of labour over the last thirty years. But if we turn to look at the way in which work has changed and workers have been reassigned within industries (as opposed to being redistributed between them) what is striking is how uniform these changes in the 'detailed division of labour' have been.

The detailed division of labour

Looking back at the history of industrial organisation we can see that every stage of the development of industrial capitalism has been accompanied by a refinement of the detailed division of labour, as capitalist entrepreneurs have striven to deploy labour in the most ruthlessly efficient way possible. Here is how Harry Braverman describes the historic process:

> In the first form of the division of labour the capitalist disassembles the craft and returns it to the workers piecemeal, so that the process as a whole is no longer the province of any individual worker. Then . . . the capitalist conducts an analysis of each of the tasks distributed among the workers, with an eye toward getting a grip on the industrial operations. It is in the age of the scientific-technical revolution that management sets itself the problem of grasping the process as a whole and controlling every element of it without exception.[14]

During the twentieth century management has employed many tools in this struggle to control every movement of the unpredictable human element in production. Attempts to motivate workers by piecework have been accompanied by time-and-motion studies that seek to calculate precisely the time a worker should be allowed to turn his or her head. More sophisticated endeavours have involved the design and utilisation of machines and systems that are not only quantitatively efficient (in that they save labour), but are also qualitatively efficient (for the capitalist), in that they discipline and regulate the movements of the worker. The conveyor belt was the first and most famous of these systems but now it is only one of many—for as semi-automation has spread from branch to branch more and more craft skills have been appropriated by the management and incorporated in masses of machinery.

As the detailed division of labour advances, the conceptualisation of work is ever more thoroughly separated from its execution. Conceptual work—the ability and freedom to imagine and plan an action before carrying it out—is removed from the shop floor to the office, and there 'a shadow replica of the process of production in paper form' becomes the basis for planning and controlling the operatives. Back on the shop floor, the human worker is reduced to the status of a machine minder and the satisfaction of creation is replaced by the numbing experience of repeatedly and endlessly performing a single set of movements day in day out. No skill, no contact, no need or basis for understanding the complete production process.

The uneven spread of electronic information technology—first applied to production in the oil, chemical and utility industries and later introduced into other branches of manufacturing—has accelerated the divide between the shop floor and the office and has tended to polarise the workforce into deskilled manual labourers (often misleadingly classified as semi-skilled) on the one hand and mental labourers in the technical, administrative and supervisory grades on the other. Squeezed in between are a declining band of skilled manual labourers—descendants of the old craft workers—who are responsible for maintenance and adjusting machines for the first runs of new products, etc. As the century has progressed, more and more of the skilled workers' functions have landed up on the office desk or in the laboratory. Thus at the turn of the century fewer than 8 per cent of workers in manufacturing industries in the principal capitalist economies were classified as not being directly engaged on production. By the end of the second world war this had risen to something like 16 per cent. By 1971 however, 27 per cent of UK manufacturing employment was classified as technical, administrative and supervisory; in the USA the proportion was 27.5 per cent and in Japan 29.2 per cent.[15] And it has not only been within manufacturing industry that the mental labourer has come to occupy an important place.

The proliferation of business and financial services and the steady burgeoning of the state bureaucracy have also brought with them a steady increase in the number of non-manual jobs available in all the major capitalist societies, particularly since the basis of office work until very recently escaped any fundamental technological transformation capable of dramatically increasing the productivity of the mental labourer. In the UK for instance the proportion of people working in offices of one sort or another rose from 30 per cent of the total workforce in 1964 to nearly 50 per cent in 1976.

This increase in non-manual jobs had important consequences on the social and political plane, particularly during the fifties and sixties—for just as the needs of various national capitals for a healthy, well-housed and educated workforce coalesced with the determination of the working class not to return to the grim days of the thirties, the changing detailed and social division of labour created opportunities which corresponded to the deeply-held aspirations of many working class parents that their children should 'do better'.

The children of working class families living in the industrial areas of Britain during the thirties would have usually expected to follow virtually in the footsteps of the previous generation, getting work, perhaps after a long period of unemployment, in one of the local industries at much the same level in the hierarchy of labour as their parents. Some of this thirties generation would have migrated to other cities if their specific locality had been particularly hard hit by the depression. Even fewer—perhaps one or two in a thousand—would have got the education or the opportunity to migrate to a job that was recognisably a step up the ladder. In the fifties and sixties this changed: not only were real wages rising but the social and detailed re-division of labour was proceeding apace. New education and job opportunities now confronted many children of the white working class. More and more men escaped the blue collar categorisation of their fathers as they got jobs in expanding occupations away from the rail depots, the mines and the factory floor.

In countries where social democratic parties were in power this reinforced their claim that they had embarked on the creation of an egalitarian society (a society, that is, where everybody would be equally free to compete in the oppressive competition of everyday life under capital) and these changes in the detailed division of labour proved to be an important factor in the parliamentary successes of social democracy. For the majority of working class children the benefits of this 'upward mobility' were—where it occurred—both real and illusory. They were real in the sense that they could escape the dirt, long hours and physical effort of the labour their parents had done and often still did. But they were illusory in the sense that departure from the factory floor did not bring any automatic escape from the dehumanisation of work brought about by the detailed division of labour. For as the amount of labour power employed away from the immediate point of production has increased, so have capital's attempts to discipline that labour. This disciplining involves not only de-skilling, as the office labour process is split into its component parts (and sub-divisions of clerical work are created to deal with purely repetitive paper work), but also the dismembering and even mechanisation of specialised white-collar functions.

Many of the jobs the (usually male) children of the working class now avoided were not themselves abolished. These jobs—together with other low-pay, low-status jobs freshly created by the expansion of the service sector and the re-division of labour in manufacturing—were filled by incorporating new groups into the workforce: by tapping new reserves of labour. It is the source and particular role of these reserves which give us an insight into perhaps the most important strand in the recomposition of the working class during the last thirty years.

Recruiting from the reserves

The crucial role played by reserves of labour in the expansion of the capitalist system was analysed by Karl Marx in *Capital:*

> The mass of social wealth, overflowing with the advance of accumulation and capable of being transformed into additional capital, thrusts itself into old branches of production, whose market suddenly expands, or into newly formed branches, such as railways, etc., which now become necessary as a result of the further development of the old branches. In all such cases, there must exist the possibility of suddenly throwing great masses of men into the decisive areas without doing any damage to the scale of production in other spheres. The surplus population supplies these masses.[16]

There is an inherent tendency within capitalist development for reserves of labour to be constantly recomposed as there are always some workers somewhere losing their jobs—this happens on a more massive scale at particular points in time (as the economy goes into recession), but it is also happening constantly as technological innovation destroys certain jobs and branches that are declining shed labour. Throughout the post-war period this 'labour shake-out' has been a very important factor in the constant creation and re-creation of the labour supply necessary to fuel expansion. However the scale of the expansion during the upswing of the fifties and sixties was so strong that it necessitated the tapping of other reserves. New workers for expanding branches of industry and the services came from three main sources—small farmers and agricultural labourers from within the country, immigrant workers from underdeveloped territories outside the central capitalist states and—in vastly increased numbers—women from the homes of the native working class. Each metropolitan country presents a distinct profile in that it drew its labour reserves more from some sources than others and used different methods to discipline them.

Contrary to the cultural images which confine them to the roles of housewife and mother, women were drawn into the paid workforce outside the home on a massive scale during the post-war boom. In the USA ten million more married women joined the payrolls in the twenty years after 1945. In Japan the number of women working outside the home rose from 2 to 12 million between 1950 and 1970. In Britain, although the increase was not so dramatic, it was a 2.2 million rise in the number of working women that was almost entirely responsible for the 2.4 million increase in the working population between 1951 and 1971.[17] In that year women made up 40 per cent of the workforce (up from 29 per cent in 1931) and five years later, in 1976, 58 per cent of all women of working age in the UK had paid jobs—33 per cent in full-time work and 20 per cent in part-time work.[18] As Irene Bruegel has noted:

> The process becomes self-fuelling. Increasingly the maintenance of family living standards has come to depend on two or more wage packets, and all adult female labour has become potential wage labour—as many as a quarter of the mothers of pre-school children are now employed.[19]

The exodus off the land was proportionately very important in Japan, Germany and France. In the USA, although the proportional change was smaller, the rural-urban transfer included nearly four million black people who left the land in the twenty years after the war. It was their journey to the northern and western cities that decisively shifted black America's centre of gravity from the rural south. The primary cause of this great wave of migration was the industrial revolution that swept through agricultural production, doing away with the need for cheap unskilled labour in first one operation, then another. The figures for output and employment can give us an idea of the extent of this transformation: between 1950 and 1965 mechanisation and the use of chemicals increased farm production by 45 per cent—in the same period total employment fell by 45 per cent. In a parallel process, a million small farms disappeared between 1950 and 1969 as new machinery and methods increased the capital required for profitable production and spurred monopolisation. This transformation had a particularly marked impact in the south where blacks coming off the land were often refused jobs on the basis of race and, throughout most of the south, were consistently denied unemployment benefits. Pushed on, the travellers usually made for the northern and western cities where there were already large black communities. Thus by 1960 half of the blacks in each of the six cities with the largest black populations—New York, Chicago, Philadelphia, Detroit, Washington and Los Angeles—had been born elsewhere, virtually all in the south. In Japan, Italy, Germany and France the workers who came off the land were not racially distinct and did not form a separate stratum of the urban working class; in the USA these migrants entered an urban labour market stratified by institutionalised racial barriers which rigidly confined them to certain jobs and sectors of the economy.

Every metropolitan country apart from Japan also drew significantly on the huge reserves of labour accumulating in overseas underdeveloped territories. In the USA immigration from the Caribbean and Central America in particular supplemented the migration to the cities. In Europe, once millions of refugees had been resettled, Germany, Holland, France and Switzerland evolved the contract labour system which allowed them to import workers without dependants on a short-term basis from countries fringing the Mediterranean. From the late fifties onwards a constant migration developed as Portuguese, Spanish, Moroccan, Algerian, Italian, Greek and Turkish workers journeyed to the central European economies. In 1976 it was estimated that there were well over 11 million immigrants in Western Europe, excluding the United Kingdom. Some twenty years before this, Britain had turned not to the European fringe but to its colonies and the independent territories of the Commonwealth for the labour it required. This source of labour became important as Irish immigration, the recruiting of contract labour via the European Volunteer Scheme, and the resettlement of refugees tailed off in the early fifties. By 1971 Britain had imported some 1.5 million workers who had been born abroad to parents also born outside the UK.

None of the new entrants into the metropolitan labour market joined or blended with a homogenous working class. They joined a working class already stratified by skill and status, by ethnic group, by colour and by sex.

The sexual division of labour is not of course capitalism's child. It is part and parcel of the patriarchal legacy that capitalist society inherited from previous eras—an inheritance which included the patriarchal family, a sex-biased legal system and sexual inequalities of income, inheritance rights and property holding. The successive and massive social transformations which have accompanied the different phases of capitalism have appropriated and modified these structures (and the sexual division of labour), but they did not create them. The sexual division of labour is all-pervasive in that it regulates the home as well as the workplace. Here we are looking at the position of women within the paid workforce, but we need to keep in mind the dual nature of women's oppression. Firstly because the nature of women's work outside the home is often conditioned by the roles they fulfil within the family. And secondly because their continuing responsibility for keeping the family unit going is one of the mechanisms which maintains the sexual division of labour within the realm of production, in that it denies many women the opportunity of taking full-time (or continuous) paid work.

The sucking in of cheap female labour has provided the basis for the expansion of the labour-intensive private and state sectors throughout the post-war period, and, as activities previously carried out within the family have become partially socialised in the market place, very large numbers of women have come to be employed in service sector jobs involving cleaning, caring, catering, nursing and teaching—occupations which reflect the traditional female role within the home. Women are also employed in large numbers as secretaries and routine clerical workers, machine-minders and assembly workers in factories, and in the lowest grades of the retail sector.

While the sexual division of labour is pervasive in that it bridges the public world of production and the private world of the home, the racial division of labour is remarkable for the general uniformity of its operation. Imperialism, bringing to fruition the creation of the capitalist world market, embraced an internationally instituted racial division of labour, since the production of agricultural and mineral raw materials was concentrated in the colonial and semi-colonial world where the workforce was paid subsistence wages. A racial division of labour was also frequently to be found in the industrialised and industrialising countries prior to this time—for instance in the USA the black slaves had already formed a distinct stratum for generations, and in England the 'cellar-dwelling Irish' had been ghettoised in jobs their English counterparts proved reluctant to take.[20] Marx and Engels, commenting on this observed how:

> every industrial and commercial centre in England now possesses a working class divided into two hostile camps, English proletarians and Irish proletarians. The ordinary English worker hates the Irish worker as a competitor who lowers his standard of life . . . he cherishes religious, social and national prejudices against the Irish worker.[21]

Then, as now, migration and racial division within the working class went hand in hand.

In the United States, and to a lesser extent in Britain, the modern racial division of labour has been dented by revolt during the last fifteen years. But this, and variations in the legal status of immigrant workers in different countries notwithstanding, there is very little difference between the central capitalist economies when it comes to the tasks fulfilled by most migrant and immigrant workers. As Castles and Kosack put it when concluding their pioneering study of immigrant workers in Europe:

> Immigrant workers in France, Germany, Swizerland and Britain are usually employed in occupations rejected by indigenous workers . . . Typically, such jobs offer low pay, poor working conditions, little security and inferior social status.[22]

In all these countries most foreign-born workers are employed in manual occupations; and construction, engineering, textiles, catering and domestic service are the branches with the heaviest concentrations of immigrant and migrant workers.

In the case of Britain, the 1977 Department of Employment report on 'The Role of Immigrants in the Labour Market' shows that:

> the main role of immigrants in the British labour market has been to provide certain industries with a relatively cheap labour pool at a time when it would have been neccessary for employers to reduce

shift hours and increase rates of pay in order to maintain and attract an indigenous workforce.

Survey after survey has shown that immigrant workers, on every conceivable criterion, are in jobs inferior to those of their white counterparts. They too have come to provide the human fuel for the expanding labour-intensive service sector. In London's restaurants, cafes and snack-bars, for example, where low pay and bad conditions are the norm—over half the workers are immigrants. Black women in Britain face a combination of racial and sexual divisions of labour, ensuring that they can generally only obtain jobs at the very bottom of the pile as cleaners, sweated workers in the labour-intensive branches of manufacturing, manual service workers doing long hours or homeworkers getting very low pay.

Swelling the surplus population

The same racist and sexist practices and mechanisms which determined where the new recruits were deployed during the long boom are also in operation during the present period—as the surplus population is swollen by stagnation and recession. Thus in situations where black and female workers are in direct competition with indigenous male workers for a declining number of jobs, it is the former who are most likely to be expelled from the workforce. But although women and racial minorities have been particularly hard hit during the last decade, the move back to higher levels of unemployment has not been effected by a simple reversal of the previous processes of recruitment: all those from the social groups that were sucked into waged labour have not been expelled en masse. For instance, branches of the economy which have been particularly dependant on black or female labour for their survival or expansion (like hotels and catering) continue to employ and even recruit more of these workers; for in the absence of developments capable of forcing sufficient numbers of male indigenous workers to accept radically reduced wages there is no other option for these employers.

Similarly, there are working class communities where male unemployment has risen far faster than female unemployment—these are generally in areas highly dependant on sharply contracting industries like steel, car manufacture and shipbuilding, which have up to now employed an overwhelmingly male workforce. Nevertheless, looking at the composition of unemployment in the central capitalist states, it is clear that disproportionately large numbers of women, migrants and members of the indigenous racial minorities have become marginalised economically as the long boom has petered out. Joining these previously employed people in the ranks of the unemployed and underemployed have been many young people—male and female, black and white—entering the labour market for the first time during a decade marked by rumbling recession.

Official figures for women's unemployment seriously underestimate its extent because many women do not register as unemployed if they are ineligible for benefit. Even so these figures show a significantly higher rate of female to male unemployment in the OECD states.[23] In Britain a more accurate indication of female unemployment rates has been reached by working from data drawn from the General Household Survey. Irene Bruegel's calculations show that between 1974 and 1976, while total male unemployment in the UK (registered and unregistered) rose by 10 per cent, total female unemployment was up by 28 per cent and the number of single women out of work rose by 42 per cent.[24] Between 1974 and 1977 the female labour force in manufacturing fell by 9 per cent, while 5 per cent of male manufacturing jobs disappeared. And it was part-time women workers who were the most readily dismissed, for in every manufacturing industry where employment declined (with the single exception of clothing) the rate of decline for part-time women workers exceeded that for full-timers, both female and male. However this sharp expulsion of women workers from manufacturing was to some extent cushioned by a continuing recruitment of female labour in the various sub-divisions of the service sector. Thus between 1971 and 1976 total female employment in industries other than those classified in the index of production (i.e. the service sector) rose by just over a million as against a rise of less than a quarter of a million in male employment. Over 80 per cent of these new jobs for women were part-time ones, and as a result by 1976 84 per cent of the close to four million women part-time workers in the UK were employed in the major service sector industries—where pay is generally lower than in manufacturing.[25]

Thus, while the seventies have brought increased overall rates of female employment, the differential impact of the crisis on the broad sectors of the economy has been to increase the proportion of women working part-time and to reinforce the concentration of women at work in the lower paid service sector industries. Where women can be exploited more effectively than men, they continue to be recruited—where they are in competition with men, they are likely to be expelled from the workforce.

Developments in the seventies also bore down hard on migrants and workers from racial minorities throughout the central capitalist economies. In France, in 1978, foreign males made up 17.7 per cent of the job seekers, although they only accounted for 9.4 per cent of the working population.[26] In the United States the unemployment rate for black workers under 20 is running at between 30 per cent and 50 per cent in the major cities. In Britain overall registered unemployment rose by 65 per cent between November 1973 and May 1975, but the number of black people signing on at the employment exchanges rose by 156 per cent. Black women appear to have lost their jobs three times as fast as white women during this period. And it is in the big cities and the urban core, as in the United States, that black unemployment is at its highest. Data from the 1977 National Dwelling and Housing Survey shows that while male unemployment in England was just below 6 per cent, and black male unemployment 8 per cent, it was over 12 per cent in Inner Lambeth and 31 per cent in Liverpool rising to 34 per cent in the city's inner area.

There has also been a massive growth in unemployment among the under 25s of both sexes. The average percentage rise of those aged 15-24 who were unemployed in France, Japan, Spain, UK and USA between 1970 and 1976 came to nearly 7 per cent and ranged from a rise of 1.2 per cent in Japan to one of 10.4 per cent in the UK. Since 1976 the position has worsened, and in 1979 across the OECD as a whole, the under 25s accounted for 40 per cent of the 16 million people officially recognised as unemployed.

We can see therefore, that with the formation of a surplus population during a long wave of stagnation, certain groups are disproportionately represented. Due to the operations of the racial and sexual division of labour, many who join the surplus population may not be able to get work in mainstream occupations. Instead they will either become the long-term unemployed or become susceptible to exploitation by archaic forms of production in the seated industries, in occupations characterised by exceptionally long hours and low pay in the service sector, or dependent on casual work and work in the lower reaches of the black economy.

The advanced industrial countries have responded to the swelling of the surplus population by attempting to limit the numbers of foreign, immigrant and migrant workers within their borders, and where politically possible expelling numbers of foreign workers from their territories. The settler status of the vast majority of black and immigrant workers in the US and UK has precluded these governments from direct explusion of minority citizens; instead they have concentrated on tightening up their immigration procedures even further. The European countries which had made most use of migrant and contract labour during the long boom have made moves towards reducing their numbers. Between 1973 and 1976 the German state is reported to have reduced the overall number of its 'guestworkers' by 20 per cent. Stringent controls have been imposed on contract workers who have had their rights to move into areas where there are already high concentrations of migrants restricted. In France, among other measures, a voluntary repatriation scheme has been started, moves have been made to abrogate the rights of resident Algerians, and the detention and summary expulsion of dark-skinned members of the working class has become a daily event.

The recomposition of the working class in relation to the changing contours of the central capitalist economies during the last thirty-five years has been both a combined and an uneven development: combined in the catholic sweep of changes in the social and detailed division of labour and in the universal sucking into waged labour of greater masses of workers; uneven in the earlier impact of certain trends in some societies rather than others, and in the distinctive profile presented by different countries in terms of the mix of new labour that was incorporated and the way in which that labour was utilised and disciplined. As we saw in the first part of this chapter, the stance of US and UK capital on the world market over the period of the long boom and, indeed, into the recession, has led to an erosion of the industrial base of these countries and a declining proportion of their labour forces working in industry. And within the national economy it has been the major conurbations of the north-eastern rim of the United States and the major conurbations in Britain which have suffered the greatest loss of industry. But it is also in these areas that the greatest concentrations of racially distinct labour have occurred. It is the combination of this feature of the US and UK economies with the way those states recruited and deployed migrant, immigrant and minority labour which explains the emergence of a severe crisis of social control in these urban areas.

As we have seen, all the major economies apart from Japan drew heavily on such labour—but only in the USA and the UK did the majority of these workers possess full democratic rights (the legal right to permanent settlement, the vote, the right to join a trade union, formal equality before the law, etc.). Market forces and the general currents of racism informing these cultures ensured the perpetuation of a previous racial division of labour in a modern form in the States, and the institution of a racial division of labour in the UK. But in neither country was this division enshrined in formal law. By contrast, in Germany and other European countries the majority of those confined by the racial division of labour have also been coralled by the contract system of labour and immigration, and the fact that they have not possessed even notional equality before the law. In the USA and the UK black people have faced racism in every sphere of daily life—just as the migrants in Europe have—but the fact that they can organise openly without becoming liable to deportation has opened up possibilities of fighting back and aided the growth of cultures of resistance and racial affirmation.

The differences between the two groups of countries are of course in no way absolute. France, for example, is in an inter-mediate position with fairly large numbers of immigrants possess-ing democratic rights of some sort. But a large gulf still separates Britain and the USA from countries like France and Germany. In the Federal Republic conditions confronting immigrant workers are such as to demand a comparison with Nazi labour con-trols—yet there has been little protest. The few migrant workers strikes have been defeated—often with the aid of the native Ger-man working class—and wholesale expulsions of redundant workers have been accomplished with comparative ease. Nowhere in Europe has racism and the struggle against it become a major political issue to the extent that it has in Britain. The reasons for this can be traced back to the hard battle fought by black people on the shopfloor and in the neighbourhood. And one precondi-tion for the maintenance of this struggle, both in the USA and the UK, has been the possession of full democratic rights: a state of affairs which has both made organisation possible and served to highlight the racism operating within society because of the clash between formal equality and actual inequality.

During the upswing of the post-war boom, recruitment of female and foreign workers played a particularly important role in firing expansion. As a result the proletariat at work outside the home corresponds even less than before to the white, manual and male stereotype revered for so long within social democratic parties and labour movement institutions. The metropolitan working class has two sexes and a multiplicity of racial origins.

The continuous process of proletarianisation—whereby greater and greater numbers of individuals in succeeding generations must sell their labour power on the market to exist—has laid the basis for new unities and at the same time thrust sexism and racism to the centre of the political stage. And the stereotype is in fact least applicable in the central and inner areas of the great capitalist cities. For here the full force of the changing social and detailed division of labour has combined with the regional and urban dynamics of the post-war period, to produce new contours of growth and decay, new patterns of employment and unemployment.

3. The Regional Dynamic

January 1936: In South Wales, particularly in the Rhondda valley, the tramp of thousands of feet was heard day after day. Even the shopkeepers closed their doors and joined the demonstrations. They knew what this new attack would mean to them, that more little shopkeepers would be driven out of business by the poverty of the people and their inability to purchase goods. Doctors also marched; they knew that the new [unemployment benefit] scales meant increased difficulties for them in their desperate efforts to protect the health standards of the people against the ravages of poverty. Teachers, who had the difficult problem of endeavouring to educate half-starved children, knew that their task would become still more onerous under the new scales, so they too joined in the demonstrations. Employed workers who found that they were being compelled to maintain their unemployed relatives out of their meagre wages, joined with the unemployed. Reactionary trade union officials who had steadfastly declared that they would not stand on a public platform with revolutionary workers found themselves caught up in the stream and carried forward to participation in great united front unemployed demonstrations.

Wal Hannington, *Unemployed Struggles*[1]

Looking back to Britain in the thirties the spatial distribution of the surplus population stands out clearly. The old industrial heartlands of Wales, the North and Scotland—where the core industries built up during the nineteenth century were seized by decline—had average rates of registered unemployment double those in the relatively prosperous South-East and Midlands regions. In Wales, for example, the proportion of the insured population unemployed averaged 30.1 per cent between 1926-36, as against 8.8 per cent in London and 11.1 per cent in the South-East region. In 1934 unemployment in most of the industrial Welsh valley towns was running at over 50 per cent. But such figures tell only part of the story—for the industrial graveyards also had more short-time working, lower female activity rates and a rising proportion of old people in their populations (as those of working age migrated in search of jobs).

The fact that a large proportion of those who had been marginalised by economic change were not only concentrated together, but also concentrated in areas where elements of a socialist working class culture were at their strongest, had important consequences on the political terrain. It allowed for the emergence of a strong organisation among the unemployed—the National Unemployed Workers Movement—which, although shunned by the official trade union hierarchies, fought continually and often successfully against benefit cuts and other punitive measures sought by the National Government. It is also likely that the NUWM's activities in organising the unemployed, and maintaining their links with the rest of the working class, was one of the principal reasons why the fascist movement never made significant headway in the depressed regions.

The entry into a long wave of stagnation in the 1970s once again severely affected the older industrialised regions of the British Isles. Closures in the steel and coal industries are threatening to snap the backbone of South Wales' industrial base. On Clydeside the shipyards have gone and massive redundancies in factory after factory have become an almost monthly event. In the North-West and North-East the slow abortion of basic industries is continuing side by side with the closure of post-war factories operating in more modern sectors of the economy. Yet despite all this, it would be a mistake to see the spatial impact of stagnation today as a mere re-run of the thirties. For instance, between 1974 and 1979, although the old depressed areas had higher levels of unemployment than the Midlands and the South-East, unemployment was rising fastest in these latter regions. Today's unemployment blackspots embrace inner areas of the London and Birmingham conurbations—the beacons of prosperity in the thirties—as well as steel towns like Corby in the Midlands, and whole cities, suburbs and towns in the older industrialised regions.

The complexity of the present spatial distribution of the surplus population stems in large part from the way in which the post-war transformation of the international and national economy has overlain and reformed the patterns of uneven development inherited from previous eras. In the course of this transformation the relationship between regions and their urban structures has been modified—a process we examine in detail through the example of London in Chapter 4. This chapter starts from a wider perspective, looking at how characteristic patterns of uneven development have emerged at different stages of the development of the capitalist mode of production; examining the attempts of the modern state to intervene in this process and the complexity of the regional patterns that have resulted from the interaction of capital's calculations and state intervention in the post-war period; and charting the impact of the present phase of stagnation in the regional and urban map of unemployment.

Capital's calculations and uneven development

From the triumph of the industrial revolution onwards, continued and constantly shifting spatially uneven development has been assured by a central feature of the capitalist mode of production. This is that a capitalist enterprise cannot in the long-run survive by simply producing an ordinary rate of profit out of commodity production. For within the capitalist mode of production the rule of competition between individual capitals holds sway, and a struggle occurs over the distribution of the spoils which are realised through the exploitation of labour. This struggle between individual enterprises leads, over long periods, to the emergence of larger and larger capitals as they defeat or subsume less profitable capitals that are unable to marshal the resources to enter the next round of the fight. The struggle to survive—to be the cannibal and not the victim—propels each enterprise to engage in a remorseless search for extraordinary or above average profits; and it is this ceaseless quest—more than any other feature of industrial capitalism—that is responsible for spatially uneven development. This inherent tendency in capitalism, which flows from the nature of the accumulation process, works itself out in historically specific ways. Thus in each succeeding epoch of industrial capitalism dominant patterns of development and underdevelopment have emerged, as the pursuit of the highest possible level of profitability has produced specific locational requirements for capital operating in key branches of the economy; and as capital operating in all branches has striven to exploit the unevenness created by previous phases of development. A brief historical sketch will clarify this dynamic.

The spread of industrialisation on a capitalist basis throughout Europe in the nineteenth century was itself aided and prefigured by a marked widening in the unevenness of development between different continents in the preceding mercantile era. During that era, Europe's increasing wealth had owed much to the plundering of other continents and the labour of slaves working plantations in the colonies. The triangular trade between the west coast of Africa, the Americas and Britain, centering on the transportation of slaves, had sped the accumulation of merchant capital in Britain. As Marx put it:

> the colonial system ripened trade and navigation as in a hot house—the colonies provided a market for budding manufactures and a vast increase in accumulation was guaranteed by the mother country's monopoly of the market, the treasures captured outside Europe by undisguised looting, enslavement and murder flowed back to the mother country and were there transformed into industrial capital.[2]

The industrial development of Lancashire stemmed in part from the colonial profits realised by the slavers of Liverpool.

With the establishment of industrial capitalism in Britain at the end of the eighteenth century, production came to be based in factories which were powered first by water and then by steam. Whilst marginal increases in the productivity of labour had been achieved in previous historical periods, the concentration of labour in factories produced a phenomenal increase in the productivity of labour over a short period. Factory owners were thus able to undercut enterprises producing by way of craft manufacture, organised through an outgrowth of the old guild system in the towns and employment of outworkers in their own cottages in the countryside.

Whenever the capitalist mode of production took root in national markets it broke through the urban, regional and social boundaries of the societies that bore it as the balance between industrial, craft and agricultural production and between town and country was swiftly overthrown. One immediate result was the reversal of the distribution patterns that had become dominant during the mercantile period. Many market towns lost their importance as centres for the exchange of goods as the spread of railways led to an increasing velocity of trade between widely dispersed regions where production was now concentrated and centralised in large units.

The new factories' three main requirements were labour, land and coal. One of the largest components in the cost of a product was that of transporting the raw materials, the coal to drive the machinery, and the finished product. Factory owners discovered that the lowest costs of production could be obtained in the growing black belts of the Midlands and the North. There, coal and iron was close at hand, land cheap and labour abundant. London, Britain's pre-eminent manufacturing centre in the previous era, was largely bypassed by this upsurge of industrial development.

Although the capital city could offer a pool of cheap labour, the relatively high level of organisation among its skilled workers—a legacy of its past position as a hub of craft manufacture—meant that they were often able to resist changes which threatened their livelihood, and thus limit the entrepreneurs' freedom to innovate and deploy labour in the most profitable way possible. In addition, commercial growth had already forced up land prices in and around the city and—most important of all—coal was being mined far away at a time when transport costs were high.

As factory production in the new sectors established itself in the industrial belts of the North, London's old established industries like shipbuilding, heavy engineering and silkweaving began to decline, swelling the supply of labour in the city and leaving a vacuum at the centre of its industrial structure. The manufacturing and processing industries that survived, and even expanded during this period, were those that reduced their costs and raised their profits and ability to compete by finding more effective means of exploiting the oversupply of labour. The most notorious means was the system prevalent in the clothing, footwear and furniture trades which became known as 'sweating'. Within this set-up the production of cheap consumer goods destined for the growing urban working class market was split into the maximum number of separate operations and 'vertically disintegrated' to small workshops and homeworkers, each carrying out one of the operations in relentless repetition. By farming out their work, the wholesalers who controlled the trades could compete with provincial factory production by cutting down their own overheads and driving down wages.

The introduction of cheap hand-driven machinery like the sewing machine and the bandsaw allowed the wholesalers to circumvent dependence on skilled labour and, because there was little fixed investment, both expansions and contractions of production could be met at little cost to the entrepreneur. Like casual labour in the docks, which spread to other forms of riverside employment during the 1860s, sweated work brought poverty wages, periodic misery and constant insecurity to those forced into it. Thus the decay created by the capitalist mode of production was itself exploited and became the basis for special branches of production employing sections of the surplus population.

With the concentration of industrial capital in factory towns and the elimination of cottage industry, wide reaches of the agricultural regions became the sources of labour required in even larger quantities by the young giant industries. By 1851 nearly 50 per cent of the 6.6 million people living in the 22 largest towns and cities in England and Scotland were rural migrants. During the course of the century the rural population fell from roughly 70 per cent to 20 per cent of the total population. As competition undermined the position of small-scale independent urban producers, many of them joined the surplus population. This wide-sweeping double movement of proletarianisation was as fitful, violent and spasmodic as it was inexorable—affecting one group or area then another. But whatever the complexities of industrial development, the dominant feature of uneven development at this time was the rapid growth of urban industrial centres on the one hand and of stagnation and regression in the agricultural regions and districts on the other. So industrial growth in Britain was centered on the industrial towns of the Midlands, South Wales, the North and Southern Scotland, while in the agricultural regions the productivity of labour was relatively stagnant, employment both on the land and in craft industries was falling and there was no commensurate increase in industrial work. At the same time, what little capital did accumulate in these declining areas was effectively drained by the banking system to be invested in the industrial districts.

Ireland was bound—by statute and force of arms—into the mainland's patterns of growth and decay. It effectively became another one of Britain's agricultural regions providing labour for industry, foodstuffs for the growing cities, recruits for the army, and rent for absentee landlords. Similar patterns of growth and decay can be found in other industrialising countries during this period of freely competitive capitalism. In Belgium the destruction of Flemish cottage industry with the advent of machinofacture led to similar results in the Flanders region; later in Italy the southern Mezzogiorno regions played the role of stoking growth in the industrial north. In America the southern states, with the economies built on slavery, were a source first of cheap raw materials and then of cheap labour, used to stimulate the development of industrial capitalism in the north-east. Zones to the east and south of the German Empire and the agricultural west and centre of France also fulfilled the function of 'internal colonies' during the establishment of industrial capitalism in these national markets.[3]

The dominant pattern of growth and decay in the nineteenth century was that of the modern factory town confronting both the sweated forms of production in London and the stagnating agricultural regions. In the inter-war period, a change to this pattern became clear—then, for the first time, there was a juxtaposition of growing and declining industrialised regions.

The staple industries which had made Britain the workshop of the world in the nineteenth century—coal, textiles, iron and steel and shipbuilding—all suffered from a drastic decline in demand and inadequate investment in the inter-war years. In the coal industry, for example, demand ceased to grow after the first world war for the first time in centuries. This was primarily because of the decline in the iron and steel trade and the growing substitution of oil for coal as a basic fuel. In addition, the consistent failure of the owners to invest in mechanisation meant that, technically, British industry began to fall behind its foreign competitors and so lose export markets. As a result output fell from an annual average of 268 million tons in 1970-1914 to 228 million tons in 1934-38.[4]

The low levels of investment stemmed from the low profitability of these sectors and the consequent flight of capital from them and into the new growth industrial sectors—the 'science based' industries. These industries, which included electrical engineering and appliance manufacture, motorcars and aeroplanes, precision engineering, pharmaceuticals and food processing, were being located in the Midlands and the South-East of England. The establishment of the National Electricity Grid during this period (completed in 1933) freed the owners of industrial capital from their dependence on the coalfields and railways and allowed them to site production away from the well-organised socialist North. Instead, they looked towards London and calculated that the capital city was much more attractive in terms of profitability than other locations. For a start, the size and relative lack of organisation of the London labour force was a decided advantage. While migration and the natural increase in population could meet the need for semi-skilled labour on the new conveyor belts, the need for skilled labour in the toolroom could be met by drawing on the pool of craft skills that still survived in London. Here, at the centre of the growing road system, was also a major port for the import of raw materials and the export of finished goods. In addition many of the new science-based industries were producing consumer goods for the middle classes.

The imposition of protective tariffs in the thirties shielded both the home market and the Empire area from outside competition. And the decline of agricultural and raw material prices on the world market brought about by the global slump also worked to the advantage of these industries, in that it released a higher proportion of middle class income for expenditure on non-staple items. Enterprises manufacturing in the Midlands and South-East could both sell their goods close-by in the large Southern Counties home market, grown fat on the fruits of Empire, and also export them through the Port of London to the white dominions.

The result of the mobility of capital between old and new industrial sectors led to a sharp regional juxtaposition of growth and decay. In 1924 the old industrial regions could claim 49.6 per cent of net output of industry whilst the new industrial regions only had 28.7 per cent of output. By 1935 both regions were level pegging at 37 per cent each of net output.[5] Within the new industrial regions the London area gained the most: a total of 532 of a net national increase of 644 new factories between 1932 and 1937 and two-thirds of new employment, despite having only a fifth of the total population.[6] The city became ringed with new suburban factories, especially on the West where industrial estates lined the roads to expanding towns like Slough and Reading and the other fast-growing major industrial centre, Birmingham.

Before 1914, London and the South had suffered the highest unemployment rates, and the industrial North the lowest. In the thirties the pattern was reversed. Between 1929 and 1936 the rates of registered adult unemployment were twice as high in the North and Wales as they were in the South. But these figures grossly underestimate the real extent of unemployment—in Wales and the North there was widescale underemployment and many women, youths and old men did not bother to sign on, since the job prospects were so bad. A more accurate reflection of the regional concentration of unemployment lies in a comparison of the ratios of those who had been unemployed for 12 months or more—9 per cent in London and the South-East—but 37 per cent in Wales.

Wherever unemployment and underemployment combined with wage and benefit cuts during the slump, the long-term decline of local income set in motion a complex process of decay that ate into the whole social fabric. The closure of basic industries hit ancillary trades and local services; unemployment forced up the need for local authority provision in places where rates were no longer being paid by industry. Higher rates then tended to deter investors; shops closed and roads cracked up; landlords refused to repair houses where the poverty of the people meant they could pay no more rent; in many areas the means test gnawed away at meagre family budgets forcing those in work to support unemployed relatives; families broke up as young people left home to avoid their parents being means-tested on their account. In the worst of the distressed areas the average age rose steeply as the young left en masse in search of work. Behind them a generation of undernourished and unhealthy children were growing up—and infant mortality reached levels which were often four times higher than those in Southern Home Counties towns. Such were the results of capital's mobility in the interwar period.

In the post-war period, the calculations necessary to maximise profitability have been greatly affected by the concentration of capital into increasingly large agglomerations; by the changes in production processes which allow management to split up and separate different steps and functions in the process; and by the growth of transnational production. The ability of large companies to split up the labour process into distinct stages which can then be sited separately takes its most dramatic form in the workings of a transnational operating on a gobal scale.

Today, investment calculations in a large corporation centre on juggling with particular mixes of factors—such as labour costs, land prices, transport costs, and political stability—and determine the siting of each function. Such complex ongoing calculations emphasise the enhanced mobility of capital in the post-war period, a fact which owes much to a feature of the transformation of the post-war capitalist mode of production—the reduction of the lifespan of fixed capital: plant, machinery and buildings. Due to the pace of technological innovation much machinery now has a 'lifespan' which is half that which existed in the thirties.[7] Relatively new machines, like computers and automated machine tools, have a life as low as five years, so a company's pursuit of maximum profits may well be best served by setting up production with state grants for five to ten years, and then moving on to take advantage of a new location, when the machinery is beginning to become obsolete and its period of tax-free allowances and rent has expired. The spatial patterns of uneven development, which have surfaced from capital's mobility, are themselves highly complex and overlay and partially dissolve the old patterns. They vary from country to country according to the history of each nation, its industrial configuration, and the strength of its economy on the world market. In Britain there has been nothing to compare with the pronounced juxtaposition of regional growth and decay that has occurred in the USA over the last forty years. The south-east states of the 'sunbelt' have come to be the favoured sites for production in the growth sectors of electronics, petrochemicals, aerospace, defence and agriculture. In addition, the sunbelt's lower rate of unionisation and wages has caused an exodus of older industries, such as paper, printing and textiles, from the north-east. As industry has expanded, so property development has followed it south, attracted not only by the above mentioned growing industry, but also by the expanding service industries of leisure, tourism and retirement. As a result manufacturing employment during the seventies has substantially increased in a number of sunbelt states and sharply decreased in the north-east.[8]

Regional economic imbalance has been present throughout the post-war period in the UK, but this pattern of uneven development was inherited from the previous era rather than laid down during the long boom. The muted nature of regional growth, in comparison to the United States, has its most basic cause in the junior position of British capital in the imperial league. But it is also a reflection of the much older British industrial structure which has been the object of successive rounds of investment, on the one hand, and the attention of the state's regional policy on the other with its declared aim of ironing out uneven development.

State policy and regional economic developments

In the post-war period every major European state has intervened in the market economy to promote growth in peripheral, underdeveloped or relatively declining regions of the national market. Such interventions amount to a form of spatial Keynesianism—for just as Keynes conceived of the state as a counterweight to the uneven and potentially disastrous movement of the business cycle, the masters of regional planning have conceived of the state as a counterweight to the politically dangerous tendencies towards regional underdevelopment inherent in capitalist progress.

Despite differences of emphasis the package of policies applied has been remarkably similar in many countries, usually being arrived at via a combination of the following elements:

(i) payment of subsidies and incentives to promote capital investment in given regions in the form of re-imbursement of a percentage of capital expenditure, interest free/low interest loans, tax allowances and the provision of low-rent/rent free factories

(ii) state encouragement of job creation in development areas via remission of employers' taxes and/or annual grants for each worker taken on

(iii) the direction of investment away from congested or prosperous areas via a licencing system or the imposition of tax surcharges

(iv) indicative planning: the preparation of structure plans plus the concentration of state infrastructure investment at given points in an attempt to implant self-sustaining growth via the creation of favourable local conditions for private investment

(v) decentralisation of state controlled investment in nationalised industries and the dispersal of employment in the state bureaucracy.

In addition to these measures designed to equalise long-term growth rates, shorter term measures have usually been taken to reduce the effects of regional disparities in household income. These have most commonly taken the form of direct income maintenance (unemployment/social security payments) and transfer payments via the central exchequer to boost the provision of services by the local state in poorer regions.

The origins of British regional policy go back to the conflicts of the early thirties. During the depth of the depression the official government line had been that the depressed areas had to work out their own salvation—as the mobility of capital was sacrosanct, the unemployed were urged to desert those areas where the owners of capital chose not to invest. To further this process, the Ministry of Labour set up formal schemes to encourage 'transference' and pushed regulations designed to make claimants move to the expanding areas.[9] A number of camps were also set up on quasi-military lines for the 'rehabilitation of the unemployed'—a move that reflected growing ruling class admiration for Mr Hitler's firm line with the German unemployed. Militant opposition to these developments—often co-ordinated by the NUWM—blocked the road to industrial conscription at a time when the hunger marches could no longer be ignored. Pressure for state intervention to stimulate industrial regeneration in the depressed areas grew as a result of mass action—and led to the appointment of two full-time Special Commissioners for the 'Special Areas'. From the start their powers were severely circumscribed and the £2 million set aside was pathetically inadequate.

It was not the Special Commissioners but rearmament that eventually brought down unemployment rates in the distressed areas. From 1936 onwards increased arms spending boosted heavy industry and new building was once again seen in the North as government arms factories were dispersed from the South for strategic reasons. In some areas however the expansion of production was held back by the high average age and ill-health of the workforce—the cumulative result of an era of near starvation wages and sustained migration of the young. At the same time the costs of congestion and a decade of sprawling uncontrolled development in the Birmingham and London regions were gradually becoming clear. The government responded by setting up an inquiry into 'the distribution of the industrial population'. Its report published in February, 1940, argued that the next peacetime government would have to introduce controls to secure a more balanced distribution of industrial growth.

The early 1940s saw a host of measures designed to ensure working class participation in the war effort: from child-care to housing, the state intervened as it had never done before. As the conflict drew to an end widespread popular determination not to return to the grim days of the thirties led to the election of the first Labour government with a parliamentary majority.

But the 1945 government was barely more radical than its forbears—as concerned as they had been to disassociate itself from any form of working class direct action, its foreign policy a masterpiece of reaction. All its major measures met with tacit approval in most ruling class circles—the nationalisation of the mines and railways, for example, were measures designed purely to improve the efficiency of the capitalist economy and had in fact been recommended by wartime working parties controlled by the Tories. It was the magnates of private industry not trade unionists who dominated the boards of the new public concerns—and the old owners receiving compensation 'beyond the dreams of avarice' were more than happy to exchange their fixed investments in declining unprofitable industries for liquid capital that could be invested highly profitably elsewhere. As with nationalisation, so with regional policy. These years saw the creation of a complex legislative framework for regional and urban planning based on the work of various committees set up by the wartime coalition. As the measures designed to achieve a more balanced spatial distribution of growth stopped well short of any attempt to take direct control over the location of industry, they met with only minor opposition from the capitalist class.

Throughout the post-war period regional policies have been important in determining the location of some projects sited within the metropolitan nations during successive rounds of investment—and they are still serving to soften the blows being dealt to employment in regions now wracked by industrial restructuring. However such interventions have never managed to have more than an offsetting effect on regional inequalities—for two main reasons. Firstly, because the post-war transformation wrenched the dynamic of regional development in ways which the packagers of regional policies either failed or never sought to control. Secondly, because monopolisation and the growth of transnational production in particular have progressively undermined the main assumptions on which regional policies were based, whilst creating a spatial division of labour within the giant corporation that has tended to reinforce regional inequalities.

The uneven impact of technological transformation during the boom years ensured that the productivity of labour grew faster in the manufacturing sector than in the service sector, with the result that the proportion of the labour force employed in manufacturing steadily decreased despite enormous increases in the volume of goods produced. Additionally, changes in production techniques and the internal organisation of the manufacturing sector ensured a steady growth in the number of technical, administrative and scientific jobs away from the factory floor. As company size increased and as telecommunications and transport systems were themselves transformed, the possibility of siting this 'office world' many hundreds of miles away from the manufacturing plant was opened up.

Given these long-term structural trends, regional policies in Britain (and elsewhere) ran against the grain of post-war growth from the very first, in that the strategy for job creation in high unemployment areas revolved around an attempt to divert manufacturing plant to designated development areas. This followed on from the (only partially correct) judgement that it was the expansion of manufacturing that was predominantly responsible for the growth of employment in the South and Midlands during the inter-war period, and led to the framing of controls and incentives which applied to factories rather than offices. As a result, even when a high proportion of new industrial building was diverted to the development areas they were still getting a relatively low proportion of new jobs—thus in the 1956-60 period the North-West, the North, Yorkshire, Scotland and Wales between them got 42.7 per cent of new factory floorspace but only 11.5 per cent of the new jobs available.[10]

Employment in business services (accounting, advertising, law, banking, insurance etc), in head offices and in the state bureaucracy—in other words in the employment growth sectors—continued to expand mainly in the most prosperous South-Eastern region and particularly at its centre in London. There the concentration of national services had a powerful 'multiplier effect' in stimulating the growth of local services and the personal service sector. After the mid-sixties, controls on office developments in the main centres were introduced, but the attempt to midwife the decentralisation of office employment led mainly to a wider dispersal within the more prosperous regions—thus 77.5 per cent of the jobs moved through the Location of Offices Bureau between 1963 and 1975 went from central London to the South-East; only 0.5 per cent of them went to Scotland, Wales and Northern Ireland combined.[11] None of the top UK companies have had offices in Scotland or Wales. The relative absence of office/service sector activities, accounting for the major national increases in women's employment, was in fact one of the factors contributing to the low average rates of female participation in the paid workforce found in the North, Northern Ireland and Wales during the sixties.[12]

A second primary feature of the post-war boom was the capital intensity of many key growth sector activities. Within this framework, it has become possible for enormous amounts of capital to be invested in highly advanced complexes in an underdeveloped agricultural or industrially declining region, without producing a significant spin-off either in terms of stimulating related use industries or producing long-term jobs for the local unskilled unemployed.

Southern Italy provides a prime example of the way in which subsidies to capital expenditure have precipitated regional 'industrialisation without development' or 'development without employment'. Italian industrialisation led to a triangular concentration of basic industries in the North-West. The South entered the post-war period with its economy firmly anchored in subsistence peasant agriculture and what industrial activity there was revolving around the declining traditional industries of tile manufacture, leather working and furniture making. From the sixties onwards the Casa per il Mezzogiorno offered enormous investment subsidies to both private and state owned companies, as a result of which the region's share of total national capital investment rose from 15 per cent in 1951 to 44 per cent in 1973. By far the largest slice of this investment went to the building of petrochemical complexes[13]—'cathedrals in the desert'—which employed highly skilled workers imported from outside the region, but very few of the local unemployed. Although at the end of the period the South was taking over two-thirds of capital investment in Italy its share of industrial employment had actually fallen from 19 per cent to 17 per cent.

Emigration to the northern regions and to other European countries continued, with the Mezzogiorno's population falling from 37.2 per cent of the national total in 1951 to 35 per cent in 1973 and the regional share of total national income declining from 24.7 per cent to 22.5 per cent.[14] Household incomes in the North-Eastern triangle remain 40 per cent above the national average, those in the South 40 per cent below it. In western Wales and on the east coast of Scotland, similar massive concentrations of fixed capital have had equally little impact on rural poverty and underemployment.

With monopolisation and the growth of transnational production in the post-war period the spatial division of labour created by the giant company has become a crucial determinant of regional development. And given the increasing percentage of the GNP controlled by the top hundred companies, state regional policy has increasingly stood or fallen on its efficacy in influencing the location decisions of a relatively small number of major companies. In Britain's case, it is now quite clear that as the post-war boom progressed monopolisation undermined the effectiveness of both stick and carrot.

The stick in question is the industrial development certificate system. Introduced in 1945, it requires companies investing in new industrial building above a certain size to obtain a licence—the theory being that when IDCs are withheld in more prosperous areas the projects concerned will be transferred to less prosperous regions where the certificates are granted automatically. In practice however most large companies that have already decided to expand in the South-East, East Anglia or Midland regions negotiate with central government secure in the knowledge that they have the power to switch their investment to other equally developed areas in the EEC—IBM is one of the companies known to have used this threat in order to get permission for expansion in the South-East of England. The increased bargaining power of the giants, together with the hostility of local authorities in the prosperous regions to the system at a time of high unemployment, has contributed to a steady decline in the number of IDCs withheld. By 1974-75 only 9 per cent of applications in the South-East and West Midlands were being turned down; by 1976-78 this had fallen to 1 per cent.[15] Evidence both from the largest companies themselves and also from independent analysis suggests that the carrots proffered by all the post-war governments have rarely persuaded major companies to do what they would not have done anyway.[16]

Incentives linked to job creation are in effect subsidies to labour costs—but given the ability of most of the top 100 companies to organise production in countries where wages are less than a quarter of the lowest UK rates, these incentives have never been enough to stem the trend towards the export of labour-intensive processes to the semi-colonial world. Even on a continental scale, the cash gains to be made by transfer-pricing, trading between subsidiaries, siphoning profits through tax-havens and the like, mean that acceptance of high investment grants to locate multi-regionally would reduce profits immediately, while hindering the process of penetrating and mopping up other national markets. All this is not to say that state incentives or controls have not had any bearing on the regional dynamic or that the giants have not invested heavily in some areas of the assisted regions—merely that they have not had a decisive effect on the spatial division of labour created by the giant company.

With generalisation of electronic information technology it has been increasingly possible for production processes to be split into autonomously functioning stages. The process of geographical separation of different functions (and of dividing skilled from unskilled 'screwdriver' work) is often precipitated by monopolisation, as the absorption of previously separate companies is usually followed by restructuring and the hiving off of different functions to other divisions of the larger whole. This process has also frequently occurred as technological innovation has overtaken a particular industry, because it is often to a company's advantage to synchronise the reorganisation of the labour process with a geographical switch.

Technological innovation generally leads to the imposition of harsher working conditions and deskilling—and is therefore likely to be opposed by the workforce. But by changing workforces completely and moving to a new plant in an area where there are large reserves of unorganised labour, companies can circumvent opposition to the introduction of new technology and raise productivity while tapping a lower paid workforce. In such transitions the post-war destination of the company has usually been a new industrial estate and the target workforce has more often than not been married women. Because the work attracted to new sites in underdeveloped or declining regions has often been that of the most deskilled kind, the progressive separation and redistribution of different production stages has had a significant incremental effect on the post-war British regional map.

During the sixties a new industrial landscape was created in the old regions of industrial decline. The state, which had turned its back on these areas during the thirties, now heavily subsidised local expenditure on housing, schools, roads and other infrastructure. With the setting up of machinery for regional economic planning during the sixties, direct and indirect state aids and incentives were concentrated at what were believed to be 'growth points' within the assisted regions. Slum clearance in the central core of conurbations like Glasgow and Liverpool was complemented by suburban development and the foundation of New Towns and greenfield site industrial complexes on the growing motorway grid. Here at least government strategists could apparently point to some conspicuous successes. US electronics transnationals—at that time still persisting in the pre-war habit of using the UK as a springboard for European expansion—were induced to make significant investments in the central Scottish New Towns; and—by contrast to the thirties—the motor industry was decentralising from London and the Midlands as Ford and General Motors opened their Halewood and Ellesmere Port plants, and Chrysler and British Leyland went to Linwood and Bathgate in Scotland.

But on every side of the glittering prizes the inequalities of regional development and disparities of average social productivity remained enormous. Estimates for the late sixties show that the product per head in South-East England was double that in Northern Ireland, a third higher than in Wales and a quarter higher than in Scotland. The South-East with its own New Towns, expanded towns and the swollen commuter belts had in fact gained a new industrial infrastructure that outstripped anything laid down in the assisted regions. With its concentration of research and development, business services, state and office employment, the London region was where many of the post-war employment growth sectors converged. Possessing an enormous pool of unskilled labour as well as skilled and educated labour aplenty it still had many advantages for industry—not least proximity to continental Europe. With its motorways, airports and modern containerports the South-East region was now increasingly linked to and affected by the powerful concentration of development in north-western Europe. In the seventies, the existence of the 'golden triangle' that has its corners at Milan,

Dortmund and Birmingham (and is a spatial reflection of capital concentration at the Common Market level) has added a further twist to the regional map.

Despite the fact that regional differences in average social productivity and rates of unemployment persisted throughout the post-war period, the new rounds of investment the regions received during the boom did not simply reproduce the old divisions inherited from previous eras. The map of each regional economy today is made up of a varying mix of new growth industries and structurally declining ones. For example, in Scotland the broad contrast created by nineteenth century industrialisation between the central industrial belt and the Highland and Borders agricultural areas still exists. Within many of the agricultural zones the vestiges of pre-capitalist craft farming persist, now often overlaid by growing tourist industry activities. Just as this is a reflection of post-war service sector expansion at the periphery, there are also some zones within the agricultural areas where the semi-industrial capital intensive farming methods of the modern era have taken hold. Adding the latest twist to this picture of the relatively sparsely populated regions of Scotland is the explosive growth of a few towns like Aberdeen which have profited from the spin-offs of North Sea oil exploration.

Within the Scottish industrial belt the contrast is between declining core industries centred on the Clyde to the east and the new growth industry branch factories set up to the centre and west. This central industrial belt is the success story of regional policy in Scotland and the cornerstone of the belt is foreign, and particularly US, investment. By 1978 US investment in Scottish manufacturing was responsible for employing 84,264 people. However this triumph of regional policy is built on a foundation of sand: 'the vast majority of these plants are satellite manufacturing plants with managements acting on instructions from the other side of the Atlantic and dependent on the US for new products.' Very little original research and development work is done, most research work is concerned with adapting US models for the European market. A recent study of the important Scottish electronics industry found that only 0.9 per cent of technically qualified staff in US-owned companies were involved in research and development. Such near absolute dependence on the foreign parent company makes a branch factory economy very vulnerable to recession, fluctuations in demand, and switches in investment strategy.

In South Wales the industrial structure includes capital-intensive investment along with modern branch factory and old declining industries. The port and refinery complex of Milford Haven has grown rapidly over the last twenty years and now handles over 30 per cent of the UK's crude oil intake, and yet there has been very little spin-off in new downstream industries and unemployment remains well above the national average. The old traditional industries to the east of Milford Haven have been running down their payrolls for some time; the Welsh coal industry employed 150,000 in the early 1950s—today it employs less than 30,000.

The Welsh steel industry's workforce had fallen from nearly 75,000 in 1970-71 to near on 40,000 in 1980. The major growth industry over this period was oil and petrochemicals, but this only employed around 12,000 workers throughout the whole of Wales. The Welsh Development Authority has made determined efforts to attract foreign capital and they now boast that Wales has the greatest concentration of Japanese capital in Europe. However almost all of this investment is in screwdriver plants assembling electronic consumer goods for the European market. Subsidies to capital are still in the main attracting poorly paid, low skill branch factory work that will itself in time become vulnerable to restructuring.

The North-East, for example, includes both a replica of Clydeside on the Tyne and one of the densest concentrations of recent capital intensive investment in the whole of Europe on Teeside. This process of new rounds of investment gradually overlaying and partially dissolving the influence of old rounds was going on in all the development areas throughout the boom. But if we measure the fortunes of these areas against the South-East region, we can see with hindsight that throughout the sixties they were in fact running in order to stand still. Even though unemployment levels were kept down, half of the total UK unemployed remained concentrated in the less prosperous regions where only a fifth of the total population lived. As a result emigration out of these regions continued, though at a much reduced rate compared to the thirties. Unemployment levels would have been much higher but for the subsidies that were encouraging the import of jobs and succouring local enterprises that, unsubsidised, would have gone to the wall. To this extent state intervention in and near the old distressed areas was offsetting the continuing rundown of employment in the traditional core industries such as textiles, steel, coal mining and shipbuilding. But it was usually skilled jobs that were going and unskilled jobs that were being provided as capital reorganised itself; thus the wives and daughters of redundant male workers were finding it easiest to get work at the beginning of the seventies. Since then the regions of already high unemployment have been hit with a series of double hammer blows as the attrition of employment in declining industries has accelerated and as the restructuring of others has swept away a sizeable number of the jobs coaxed in to the assisted areas during the boom.

Merseyside provides a prime illustration of the impact of this private sector restructuring and reveals exactly how frail the foundations of post-war growth built on subsidies to private capital prove to be in a time of recession. In the decade to 1972 the central districts of the Liverpool conurbation experienced a net loss of 72,000 jobs as port employment ran down and new investment was focused on the expanding manufacturing and residential suburbs of Speke, Huyton, Kirkby and Skelmersdale. By the early seventies unemployment in Liverpool's urban core was a nationally recognised problem and the first generation of Home Office inner city experts were using the Toxteth district as their stamping ground. But with the recession came a new phenomenon—major closures in the New Town belt.

In 1976 Courtaulds, the largest employer in Skelmersdale, closed down its factory with a loss of 1,000 jobs, soon to be followed by a shut down at Thorn's colour TV factory. Worse however was to follow with major companies like Lucas, English Electric, Leyland and Birds Eye axeing over 14,000 jobs in the Merseyside metropolitan area during 1978. In the first two months of 1979 Dunlop closed at Speke with a 2,400 jobs loss, Plessey made 1,000 redundant and the government refused further aid to the Kirkby Workers Co-op. When this closed another 700 were on the dole in the nightmare New Town where recognised unemployment was running at 25 per cent—roughly double the average for Merseyside as a whole.

The regional and urban unemployment map

The spatial distribution of the unemployed section of the surplus population is not as clear-cut as it was in the thirties. Wide regional variations in unemployment rates still exist—and the decline of employment in the state-owned shipbuilding, steel and coal industries is being felt most keenly in the traditionally high unemployment regions. In addition private sector corporations, faced with the need to cut capacity, have been closing or axing jobs in a large number of branch factories—many of which are located in areas of already high unemployment. Yet despite these trends, the substantial rise in overall UK unemployment (from an average of 2.1 per cent of the workforce between 1965 to 1969 to an average of 5.7 per cent between 1977 and 1979), has not been accompanied by a widening of regional rates of unemployment similar to what occurred during the middle years of the inter-war period. It is the widening of unemployment rates between free-standing towns and the suburban belts of the major conurbations on the one hand, and the inner urban cores of those same conurbations on the other, that has become the most obvious feature of the spatial impact of this long wave of stagnation.

As a region, it is Northern Ireland which exhibits the classic features of the distressed areas of the thirties: in October 1980 it had an adult unemployment rate of 14.3 per cent. Of all the UK regions it has the lowest gross domestic product per head; the lowest level of consumption of major consumer goods; the shortest life expectancy; the lowest average weekly wages (some 8 per cent below the South-East); and over 10 per cent of the working population have been registered unemployed throughout the last four years. This level of unemployment has continued to exist despite the combination of low wage levels and the fact that the highest subsidies to capital investment in Europe are on offer in the region.[17] The full desperation of the government's attempts to attract investment to the region were revealed in August 1978 when the Northern Ireland Development Agency put together a package of £52 million for Delorean to set up a car factory in a 'no-man's-land' area of West Belfast. In effect it was putting up two-thirds of the capital for a project already rejected by most of the world's motor industry and outbidding the development authorities of Texas, Pennsylvania, Detroit, Puerto Rico, Spain and Southern Ireland to the tune of £20 million. The factory will provide 2,000 jobs.[18]

But despite the fact that the average unemployment rate in Northern Ireland is three times that for the South-East, and that in the North, North-West, Wales and Scotland double that in the South-East, the last half of the seventies did not see a widening of differentials in regional unemployment. As Table 3 shows the rate of increase between 1975 and 1980 was remarkably uniform. And as unemployment began to rise sharply in 1979-80, the greatest percentage increases did not occur in Northern Ireland, Wales, Scotland and the North—the four regions with the highest proportion of the workforce on the dole. It was, in fact, the East and West Midlands which experienced the greatest rise in unemployment: 68 per cent and 60 per cent respectively between October 1979 and October 1980 as against 48 per cent for the UK as a whole.

Table 3: Registered Unemployed by Region as a Percentage of Workforce*

	1970–74	1975	1977	Oct† 1979	Oct† 1980	Percentage increase 1975–80
South-East	1.8	2.6	4.3	3.5	4.6	43.5
East Anglia	2.3	3.3	5.0	4.3	5.5	40.0
East Midlands	2.4	3.4	4.8	4.5	6.2	45.2
West Midlands	2.5	3.8	5.4	5.1	7.4	48.6
South-West	2.9	4.5	6.6	5.5	6.5	30.8
Yorkshire & Humberside	3.2	3.8	5.3	5.4	7.3	47.9
North	4.9	5.4	7.6	7.9	9.9	45.5
North-West	3.6	5.0	6.8	6.6	8.9	43.8
Wales	3.9	5.2	7.4	7.4	9.7	46.4
Scotland	4.9	4.9	7.6	7.4	9.4	47.9
Northern Ireland	6.7	7.3	10.1	10.5	12.7	42.5
UK Average	3.0	3.9	5.8	5.4	7.0	44.3

*Excluding school leavers

†Seasonally adjusted

Source: *Department of Employment Gazette.*

One qualification needs to be set against these trends that point to a relative convergence of regional rates of unemployment. This is that during 1979, as the after-effects of the mild recovery of 1977-78 fed through into lower unemployment figures, the greatest falls in the numbers out of work occurred in the relatively prosperous regions. Thus in the year ending August 1979—the point at which unemployment once more began to rise—adult unemployment fell by 9.1 per cent. Above average falls occurred in the South-East (15.1 per cent), East Anglia (14.5 per cent), the South-West (12.6 per cent) and the East Midlands (11.3

per cent). In contrast, unemployment only fell by 1.5 per cent in Scotland and 2.9 per cent in Northern Ireland. Clearly, as of the late seventies, the regions with lower overall unemployment rates remained more responsive to the sort of hesitant and uneven recoveries in economic activity that are likely to punctuate recession during the coming decade. Reflecting this, those out of work for over a year accounted for 31 per cent of the total unemployed in October 1979 in the North, but only 22 per cent of the total in the South East.[19]

It is when one turns from the differences between regions to the patterns within regions that the major feature of the present map of the regional and urban distribution of unemployment emerges. In 1977 officially recognised unemployment in the North-West was running at 6.8 per cent overall; but it was a good deal higher, at 10.7 per cent in the Merseyside Metropolitan County. And in Liverpool itself, work done on the National Dwelling and Household survey shows that the rate of male unemployment in that year was over 15 per cent and nearly 18 per cent in Inner Liverpool. These patterns are present in every region and bear witness to the primary feature of uneven development that has been in the ascendant in post-war Britain—namely the growth of the suburbs and smaller cities ringing the conurbations, the relative decline of economic activity in the conurbations and growing dereliction in their inner cores. This urban/suburban split has not reproduced itself evenly throughout the various regions of the United Kingdom because the regional and urban dynamics are not independent entities but interact to produce distinctive profiles of local economies. Thus not all suburbs or inner cities have been equally affected by restructuring in the seventies—the urban areas of the North-West and the New Towns of the Scottish industrial belt have been hit far harder by closures and redundancies, for example, than have the suburbs and New Towns of the South-East and the Midlands.

Where regional rates of unemployment are high they serve to cut down still further job opportunities for the inner urban working class. In London, for example, manual workers who have lost their jobs are more likely to be able to turn to travelling out into the relatively prosperous region in search of work. But in many working class communities in the areas surrounding Glasgow and Liverpool the unemployment rates are now rivalling those in the inner core. It is also generally true that where regional rates of unemployment are high the unemployment rate in the inner urban core will be correspondingly higher than the inner city unemployment rate in conurbations sited in more prosperous regions. Even so the complexity of the patterns of growth and decay brought about by the post-war transformation should not mask the fact that a pronounced build-up of the unemployed section of the surplus population has already occurred in the conurbations.

In summary then, the map of unemployment in Britain today reflects the fact that regional economic imbalance has continued to exist along the lines of the pattern of uneven development inherited from the previous era. This pattern, however, has been modified as a result of successive rounds of investment laid down under the influence of the calculations of capital in the post-war period, which have themselves been influenced by state interventions nominally designed to counteract tendencies towards uneven regional growth. Such interventions have not been able to prevent the re-emergence of much higher levels of unemployment in the old distressed areas, and in that sense they have failed.

But the success or failure of such policies cannot be measured from the state's point of view merely in terms of whether regional growth rates have been equalised. For the fact that wide sections of the British working class in areas of high unemployment continue to look to the state for an answer to the problems created by capital mobility, shows these interventions have had considerable success on the political terrain.

4. London—The Urban Dynamic

From the first throes of industrialisation to the middle of the present century what are now the London, Clydeside, Merseyside, West Midlands, Tyneside and South-East Lancashire conurbations gained population in each successive decade. Accounting for less than 3 per cent of the total land area they still house roughly a third of Great Britain's population—but since the mid-sixties the cities on which they are centred have all been losing population quite rapidly.[1] In the decade to 1976 this population decline ranged from 22 per cent in the case of Liverpool to 8 per cent in that of Birmingham as people moved to the fringes of the conurbations or well beyond into the surrounding regions.

But this migration was not a uniform one in terms of class; effected largely through the operations of the private house market, and to a lesser extent through state decentralisation policies it was households with skilled manual male wage earners that tended to move out and those with 'unskilled' and 'semi-skilled' heads of household that tended to stay behind. It is the people who have remained in the older working class areas of the major cities, together with new entrants to the British labour market and those excluded from it for reasons of age and family responsibilities, who have borne the brunt of the changes that have overtaken the urban economy. From these groups is drawn the surplus population of the older urban areas, which—as we are arguing—is both swelling in size and becoming an increasingly distinct social group within society.

It is a characteristic of long waves that patterns of development and underdevelopment that have been laid down (or continued to exist in muted form) during the expansionary phase register with full force at the surface of industrial, social and political life during the succeeding phase of stagnation. In the last chapter we saw something of how this operated in the inter-war period at the regional level. Here we are going to concentrate on how the mobility of capital has interacted with the changing social and detailed division of labour to affect the industrial structure and class composition of London. What follows analyses this in terms of large-scale manufacturing, the small firm, office and 'growth service' work, and other service sector employment. The chapter ends with a more detailed look at unemployment and the surplus population.

The decline of large scale manufacturing

In 1951, when manufacturing accounted for 35.5 per cent of total employment in Greater London, there were over 1.55 million people at work in the sector.[2] By 1966 the number had declined to just under 1.33 million, accounting for 29.5 per cent of all jobs, but this fall had been more than compensated for by increasing employment in other sectors. As a result total employment in the conurbation had actually risen from 4.29 million to 4.43 million despite a decline in population from 8.30 million to 7.81 million. Since then, however, employment in London manufacturing has fallen precipitously. Between 1966 and 1974—a period in which the city's population fell by 9.4 per cent and manufacturing employment nationally declined by 8.4 per cent—the conurbation lost 27 per cent or 370,000 of its manufacturing jobs. And the available evidence suggests that the trend has continued—the GLC for example, (in an assessment made before the extent of the 1980-81 recession became apparent) estimated that in 1981, of a total 3.70 million jobs in London only .74 million or 20.1 per cent would be in manufacturing.[3]

It is worth noting that the decline has not been localised in terms of London's 'inner city' areas. Detailed analysis has shown that there was only a couple of percentage points difference between the average rate of job loss in the inner and outer boroughs over the 1966-74 period.[4] This major rundown of manufacturing employment is a process affecting the whole conurbation—and all the major conurbations in the UK.[5] Between 1971 and 1976, for example, Liverpool lost 14 per cent of its manufacturing jobs and this was followed by 20,000 notified redundancies (equivalent to 22 per cent of the 1976 workforce) between 1977 and 1979.[6]

TV and press—drawing selectively on snippets of specialised reports and freely on the pronouncements of business pressure groups—have popularised a highly distorted understanding of this process. We are told that high rates and hostile planning decisions have killed off enterprises and that firms have been forced to leave because of the unco-operativeness of their existing workforces. A more accurate picture emerges if we look at the way monopolisation and technological transformation have altered the locational and labour requirements of leading firms and sectors.

During the nineteenth century industrialisation went hand in hand with urbanisation as industrial investment was drawn towards existing towns and cities or towards areas with special advantages (such as proximity to raw materials) which thereafter were rapidly built up. In these centres the higher costs of land—a reflection of market pressure—were offset by economies arising from other factors: the availability of labour, access to the market and—in an era when transport costs were relatively high and most enterprises were relatively small—proximity to other independent enterprises forming part of the chain of production. The interaction of all these ensured that while firms often moved to the fringes of urban areas in search of cheaper sites they rarely detached themselves from existing industrial centres. The very process of industrialisation led to urban 'agglomeration'.

During the twentieth century, however, particularly since the war, the advantages of operating within the major conurbations have been eroded and in many sectors the balance has tipped decisively against it. As monopolisation has advanced there has been a strong tendency for corporations to integrate complex chains of production on a more highly automated basis within a single plant. A prime locational requirement of these new high productivity plants is horizontal space for conveyor belts, machine to machine linkages, storage, container lorry docking, staff parking and steady expansion. But parcels of land on a scale sufficient for such major investments are not easily assembled in already built-up areas. And the most modern technology cannot be installed or profitably operated in plants cobbled together out of old multi-storey buildings which are cramped and have difficult access. (70 per cent of industrial buildings in Greater London are multi-storeyed compared to 15 per cent in the rest of the South-East.)[7] At the same time as monopolisation has reduced the need to be near clusters of suppliers, land prices have encouraged dispersal, not only because land is cheaper outside the cities but also because of the value of the urban sites if sold for redevelopment. Such asset stripping has been a factor throughout the post-war period, but became a major influence on company planning during the property boom of the early seventies.

The growth of new transport systems, and access to them, has had a decisive bearing on the location of certain types of investment. In the case of the petrochemical industry, for example, the development of seaborne bulk transport and the need for these highly capital-intensive ships to achieve a quick turnaround time determined a move from the fringes of conurbations like London to often remote deep water access ports. But across a broad range of manufacturing activity it has been the dramatic shift from rail to road haulage and the differential development of the motorway system that has been the most important influence.

Britain's motorway building programme began late in 1957, but by 1970 trunk routes running through open country and linking the outskirts of most major industrial centres had been completed. The South-East Lancashire and Birmingham conurbations had the beginnings of a system of urban motorways as well, but little progress had been made on the 1964 plan to build three concentric motorways linking areas inside built-up London to the national grid. The high cost of urban motorway building, cutbacks in capital expenditure programmes and increasingly organised opposition to the necessary clearances and the prospects of pollution, interacted to stall the plan. As a result the motorway system petered out at the edges of the capital and, at the few points where it penetrated further, merely served to feed a growing volume of traffic on to an already congested road network.[8]

In 1973, at the beginning of a period which also saw the axing of Maplin superport-airport and the Channel tunnel, plans for the two inner ringways were finally scrapped. Thus throughout the post-war period there has been a generally widening gap between the effective one day operating radius of lorries based in London and those based in other smaller cities and towns with easy access to the high speed trunk routes. And this gap has had a proportionately greater influence on location—especially for transnational companies—as the older transport systems (the railways and the upstream ports) based on the nineteenth century conurbations have decreased in importance and as traffic to and from Europe across the 'motorway bridges' provided by the east coast ports has increased.

Although some areas in the north and west of London are not as badly isolated as inner urban areas in its south and east (and proximity to Heathrow is a positive advantage in the west), there is little doubt that higher transport costs have combined with higher land prices to generally repel investment in new high productivity plants.

In terms of the availability and pliability of labour the advantages offered by London in the inter-war period were steadily eroded during the post-war boom. The growth industries of the thirties had been attracted to the metropolis by its reserves of craft labour, the size of the unskilled labour market and the comparatively low level of unionisation. By the end of the thirties some of the difficulties facing the unions in the vast city had been overcome, but even so major factories like Ford at Dagenham were not effectively organised until the fifties. During the long wave of expansion, however, demand for workers in other sectors of the capital's economy and an unemployment rate consistently below the national average combined to produce periodic shortages, encourage unionisation and raise wages. And although no precise London figures are available it is probable that by the beginning of the seventies—when over 60 per cent of the manu-facturing workforce nationally were organised[9]—the below aver-age level of unionisation that had previously attracted investors had been transformed into an above average one.

The demise of the London docks provides a clear example of how labour organisation has often spurred both technological change and spatial reorganisation. In 1967, after eighty years of struggle, the dockers finally achieved 'decasualisation' and a guaranteed minimum wage, so bringing to an end a system of employment that had provided companies with a cheap flexible labour force easily shed during slack periods. While this system had survived the employers had judged investment in 'contain-erisation' to be uneconomic. Now it followed on a massive scale and, when combined with removing the work of stuffing and stripping the containers to inland depots, resulted in the registered dock labour content of handling cargo being reduced by up to eighteen times from its previous level. In addition employers began to divert freight through ports where the Dock Labour Scheme did not apply and where companies retained unilateral control. Throughout the seventies the tonnage handled by these ports increased vastly, while the London port found itself trapped in a spiral of falling traffic and rising debt which had resulted in the near total closure of the upstream docks by the end of the decade.

For industrialists generally, the effects of increased unionisa-tion were compounded by shortages in London of tappable reserves of married female labour. As we saw in Chapter 2 the incorporation of married women into the labour force was a major feature of post-war expansion throughout the capitalist economies—in Britain over the twenty year period to 1971 a 10.6 per cent rise in the total labour force was largely the result of a 115 per cent rise in the number of economically active married females, whose numbers increased from 2.7 to 5.8 million.

In London, however, the level of women's employment was much higher than elsewhere; sufficiently large reserves of married women wishing to work, and having the childcare facilities to do so, simply did not exist. In 1951 the Greater London activity rate for married women was 39.8 per cent at a time when it was 17.3 per cent for Great Britain outside the major conurbations. By 1971 the decentralisation of manufacturing employment and the expansion of the service sector in the rest of the country had narrowed the gap: the London rate had crept up to 48 per cent, but the rate for the rest of Great Britain outside the big cities had leapt to 40 per cent. And there is strong evidence from the intervening period that it was shortages of women workers that motivated relocations triggered by labour shortages—the Department of Industry inquiry into locational attitudes during the 1964-67 period, for example, revealed that one firm in nine considered that a shortage of female labour was the 'outstanding' reason for moving; shortages of male labour were rarely mentioned despite the fact that 40 per cent of respondent firms cited labour shortages as a 'major reason' for investing in new areas.[10]

On the other hand the now frequently heard assertion that shortages of skilled labour have been a major long-term influence on the decline of manufacturing in London does not bear serious examination. One of the most thorough empirical analyses of recent changes in a given branch of British industry provides useful evidence on this. For their *Industrial Restructuring Vs. The Cities* Doreen Massey and Richard Meegan surveyed firms involved in the 1966-72 IRC-encouraged reorganisation of the electrical, electronic and aerospace equipment sectors.[11] By the beginning of the period many of these enterprises had lost markets to overseas competitors, profits were falling and overcapacity was beginning to manifest itself. A series of major takeovers took place and all the surviving firms were faced with the need to reorganise production on a more modern basis. Generally, this involved moving towards mass production techniques via the substitution of less skilled labour and semi-automatic machinery for craft labour wherever possible. Total employment declined by 16 per cent—but this figure masks a much bigger shift from skilled to semi-skilled work on the shop floor and an extensive relocation of mass production from older urban areas to greenfield sites outside the conurbations. Greater London, Liverpool, Manchester and Birmingham—which, at the beginning of the period, accounted for 32 per cent of total employment—experienced 84 per cent of the total job loss as the labour-intensive inner city plants employing a high proportion of skilled labour were axed. In this case industrial capital was not moving on because of a shortage of skilled labour—indeed it would seem that investment was often being decentralised in the expectation that the old workforce would resist the necessary deskilling. Shortages of specific types of skilled labour may well now be acting as a barrier to expansion in some inner city areas because of the long-term effects of population dispersal, the collapse of the apprenticeship system and the destruction of pools of craft skills—but to cite this as a major cause of the decline of manufacturing in the conurbations in plainly wrong. The dominant thrust of the post-war redivision of labour within manufacturing has had the effect of deskilling the workforce and it has been the search for malleable unskilled labour, not the pursuit of elusive craft skills, that has motivated the typical post-war industrialist.

Since 1976 government attempts to stem the tide in inner urban areas have involved the reversal or cancellation of policies intended to encourage the decentralisation of population and employment. These moves, and the attendant publicity, have had the effect of deflecting public attention from the degree to which the decline of the manufacturing sector in London has resulted from a process of restructuring determined by market forces and controlled by monopoly capital rather than the state. As a corollary of this, the proposition that 'bad government' has been a cause of the inner city jobs crisis has gained ground, as has the notion that the correct mix of measures conceived in the mould of post-war regional policies will solve the problem. Those that pursue this line point on the one hand to harsh planning regulations which, it is claimed, have had the effect of repelling investment and driving out (or even into bankruptcy) existing enterprises; on the other hand they point to state support for the new and 'expanded' towns and the incentives on offer in the assisted regions.

It is undoubtedly true that rolling redevelopment slum clearance programmes have displaced large numbers of small businesses, many of which have folded after being unable to find comparable premises because of spiralling rents/land prices; it is also true that planning regulations have weeded out 'non-conforming' businesses from garages and converted basements in residential areas—although the numbers involved here are probably much smaller. However where such interventions have proved to be a killer blow it is almost certain that the enterprises involved were already operating at the margins of profitability.

This being so, their chances of survival were not great in any case. And although bureaucratic delays are often cited by business groups, we have been able to find no evidence that planning regulations (rather than land prices, labour supply etc.) have been a crucial factor in persuading expanding companies to disinvest. Similarly, had market forces continued to militate in favour of urban agglomeration, it is quite clear that the big battalions would have been able to penetrate the IDC system, given the ease with which they have been able to circumvent negative controls in order to invest in the rest of the South-East region.

Nevertheless the decentralisation of employment and population from the London region did remain on the books as a major positive objective of regional/urban planning from the immediate post-war period until 1976 when central government cut back the New Towns programme and the GLC followed suit with the expanded towns schemes. The strategy dates back to the 1945 Abercrombie plan which, based on the assumption that with economic growth urban sprawl would automatically continue unchecked unless counteracted by the state, had recommended that over a million people should be dispersed to satellite towns beyond a 'green belt' where a ban on development would serve to halt the capital's outward march.

Between 1946 and 1949 corporations were set up to pilot the growth of eight New Towns for London and in 1967 Milton Keynes and Peterborough were added to the list. Financed by the state but subject to no local democratic control, these corporations carried out housing programmes, basic infrastructure development and used a variety of methods from advertising to indirect subsidies in order to attract industry to the new 'communities'. In fact the direct transfer of existing employment to the new and expanded towns was only a minor factor in London's manufacturing decline, and a lesser one than movement to 'unapproved' destinations. But these substantial programmes of investment did serve to further reinforce the advantages of all towns outside the conurbation where the availability of premises was matched by good access. In addition, the procedures adopted for allocating public housing often allowed firms to carefully pre-select a workforce from the mass of applicants on the housing waiting lists. Thus state intervention greased the path for decentralisation of manufacturing investment at a time when technological transformation and other market forces were already determining the process—a process that the state influenced, but never controlled, directed or appreciated the extent of until after the event.

The simple answer to those who have argued that the decline of London's manufacturing resulted from misconceived planning strategies is, in the words of *The Economist:* 'all major cities in Britain and the industrialised West are decentralising ... even though in most of these countries dispersal has not been a positive planning objective.'[12]

Table 4: Composition of Industrial Decline in Greater London 1966–74

loss due to movement to assisted areas		
of manufacturing employment decline	=	9%
movement to overspill towns	=	7%
unplanned movement	=	11%
firms over 20 employees		
residual shrinkage	=	21%
difference between openings and closures unassociated with movement	=	44%
decline of employment in firms with less than 20 workers	=	7%

Source: Dennis[13]

As Table 4 shows, analysis of data drawn from the Department of Industry registry of plant openings and closures leads to the conclusion that the net difference between births and deaths—in other words the excess of jobs lost through plant closures unassociated with movement, over jobs created via new investments—was primarily responsible for job loss during the period when London's manufacturing decline was accelerating. These figures are not without their problems because they relate to plants rather than corporations: it is quite possible that the axing of jobs in one company in London, although apparently unassociated with the creation of jobs in a new plant owned by a company elsewhere, is in effect a direct transfer of jobs flowing from the investment strategy adopted by the multi-divisional corporation that owns both of them. But the data in Table Four does accord with a picture of capital mobility leading to a major new juxtaposition of industrial growth and relative decline in the post-war period—the full significance of which only became apparent as slowing growth and falling profits intensified the process of selection. This pattern embraced a gradual geographical separation of dynamic and stagnating sectors as the flow of investment into some of the key growth sectors of manufacturing and processing consistently favoured sites outside the conurbations, while declining sectors remained anchored to their original locations; it also embraced a polarisation within given branches of production between leading and lagging enterprises, as those increasing their competitive edge decentralised to non-urban locations. As the uneven process of technological transformation and product innovation progressed, it also resulted in an increasingly discernible contrast between different plants under common ownership as high productivity production techniques and expanding lines were diverted to plants outside the major cities.[14] As successive cycles of investment increased the strength of the base elsewhere, the conditions were maturing for an acceleration of job loss as the pressures towards rationalisation grew in the late sixties.

As we enter the eighties, London, like other major urban centres, still has a significant manufacturing base, but total employment is half what it was tenty years ago and the current recession is showing that the process has far from run its course. In addition, manufacturing job loss has been accompanied over the last twenty years by the loss of some 400,000 jobs in 'other industries and services.'[15] Much of this job loss has been directly linked to the erosion of the city's manufacturing base (as demand for related services has been hit) or to processes of technological transformation (in the utilities, for example) comparable to those that have altered the labour and locational requirements of industrial capital.

Small business and labour intensive manufacturing

A lot of dead wood has been hacked away, but this does not mean that a healthier tree has been left behind. Just as in the 1860s, one effect of the exodus of dynamic sectors has been to increase the competition for work and facilitate the survival of relatively archaic forms of production, which have become proportionately more important in terms of total manufacturing activity in the capital. Clothing provides an example. It is a labour-intensive industry—accounting for 3 per cent of output nationally but 6 per cent of manufacturing employment[16]—operating in the face of severe competition from low wage economies and thus highly dependent on paring wage costs to the bone.

The industry's structure is sharply divided between some 500 larger firms—accounting for over half of output and employment—and over ten times this number of small firms. In this latter group a high bankrupty rate is offset by an equally high rate of new enterprise, it requiring little capital to set up in the clothing business. London remains an important centre of the industry, but the size of its firms is well below the national average—p rimarily because a significant number of larger firms, which moved out from the central areas to the new working class suburbs during the inter-war period, have since decentralised to other towns and regions. Those that remain draw on an almost exclusively female and/or immigrant workforce, raise the rate at which they exploit their workers via the piecework system, and use homeworkers wherever possible to reduce overheads. For Bengali and Cypriot small businessmen striving to make it in a racist society, the industry provides a refuge on the margins of a highly monopolised economy—but for those forced to work in it the industry means bad conditions, long hours and a grinding routine.

Small workshop production also survives in other sectors like furniture making and there is undoubtedly a lot of hidden homeworking in London, not only in the clothing trades but also in toy manufacture and the finishing and packaging of a wide range of consumer goods. Recent figures are difficult to obtain and it is too early to talk with any certainty about a 'resurgence of sweating'. However it is clear that the decline of mainstream manufacturing is interacting with other developments to swell the potential labour supply for enterprises which are linear descendants of the nineteenth century finishing trades, and also for small businesses competing against larger, more highly capitalised enterprises in more modern branches.

Grunwicks, the North-West London firm which became the focus of one of the most bitter unionisation battles of the seventies, is perhaps the best known example in the category.[17] It competes in the mail order film processing market, dominated by such giants as Kodak, where speed is a prime consideration for the typical customer, and the volume of work is subject to enormous seasonal fluctuations. While the actual processing of films is carried out, as in other firms, by high speed technology, Grunwicks has been unable to invest in sophisticated equipment to carry out the administrative/handling work required by a mail order business. In order to get this done at minium cost, with maximum seasonal flexibility, the firm drew on a mostly Asian and West Indian female workforce, which it paid little and sought to bludgeon into accepting long periods of compulsory overtime at short notice and little more than the paltry basic rate. It was in order to maintain this flexibility—and thus to be able to maintain a competitive position in a highly monopolised market that the firm's owners were prepared to fight such a protracted war against union recognition.

Grunwicks is an example made famous by street battles, but it is far from the only manufacturing firm in London dependent on the advantages of exploiting an unorganised workforce in order to stay in the competitive race. In its essential features it is just the sort of small business that has figured so prominently in both Tory and Labour government rhetoric about national industrial regeneration in recent years. In Britain as elsewhere, government began to cling somewhat desperately to the notion that the small business is beautiful after the 1974-75 recession. Since then appeals for 'initiative stifling red tape' to be cut have been followed by harder hitting demands that small firms should be exempted from employment protection and health and safety legislation.

Support for small business has also become a staple part of state strategy to halt the decline of employment in the inner city: both within the 'partnership programmes' evolved under the Labour government, and in terms of the Tory government's 'enterprise zones', where planning controls are being relaxed and exemption from local taxation is being offered to entrepreneurs. For all these reasons, it is important to understand the role that the medium and small manufacturing enterprise plays within the developed capitalist economy.

In the growth sectors, the giants have barely been troubled by the attentions of small business in the last thirty years. The sheer volume of capital required to develop new products and set up shop in these sectors prevents all but the largest groupings even contemplating the exercise. For instance, a petrochemical plant designed to produce just one main product now costs upwards of £250 million. Small and medium enterprise cannot generate such funds internally—and, given the inter-penetration of banks and existing large groupings—funds are hard to come by when the purpose of raising them is to challenge established enterprise in some of the most profitable sectors of the economy. At the same time the vast costs of reorganising production on a more modern basis within established industries has reinforced the trend to monopoly robbing small capital of its previous role as technological innovator.[18]

The expansion of the giant firm has dramatically curtailed the room for manoeuvre of small capital in the manufacturing sector as a whole. However, it would be inaccurate to represent this dynamic as simply one of pushing small firms to the edge of the cliff and then over. In many sectors the largest firms have refrained from extending their grasp to the very limits of the industry and have kept small businesses alive by tucking them into their back pockets via the sub-contracting system. This system whereby large companies are supplied with components from, or farm out work to, smaller enterprises has many attractions for companies occupying a controlling position in any given industry. They will often be the only market for the finished products of the small firms and they are thus able to impose stringent terms. In the event of fluctuations in demand the large firm is not forced to lay-off members of its own unionised workforce, but is able to diffuse possible confrontation by passing it down the line to the sub-contractors, where workers are often unorganised. Within these small firms the exploitation of labour is generally far more intense, but the effect of this shows up in the profit returns of the large company that has maximised its room for manoeuvre by integrating low-cost elements into the modern production process.

Post-war Japan provides the clearest example of this 'dual economy' arrangement in operation, although it is a system that is now coming under increasing strain. Thirteen major integrated corporations effectively monopolise the commanding heights of industry, commerce and finance. The majority of their direct employees are employed for life, recruited straight from school and organised in company unions. Their wages will usually be at least double those of less permanent workers and increase substantially according to length of service. This is an effective antidote to militancy, especially as large groupings have a common agreement not to employ a permanent worker who has been sacked by another enterprise. In return, it has been understood that the company will not lay off permanent workers whatever the state of business. The rigidity that this introduces into company wage bills is countered by taking on a class of temporary workers—these are paid less, employed on low-status jobs and can be easily dismissed. In addition even the largest companies make extensive use of the sub-contracting system. In 1960 firms employing less than 200 workers accounted for 60 per cent of the manufacturing labour force. These small firms were concentrated

103

in two sectors: the old industries of food preparation, textiles, clothing and porcelain in which they produced the final product from their own raw materials, and those industries with a more modern composition in which they functioned as sub-contractors carrying out labour-intensive production steps. Examples of this are to be found in large numbers in electronic consumer goods, auto, shipbuilding, machine tool and electric power industries. The giant companies' use of the subcontracting system:

> provokes a transfer of the risks and costs of economic fluctuations to the unprotected small firm sector in which labour is much more mobile. Small firms for their part can if necessary slough off surplus labour into the semi-activity of worthless agricultural labour. Thus the solidarity of the peasant family is what finally bears the costs of the system. In an economy where, in what would appear to be an irreconcilable contradiction, a rigid system of employment co-exists with violent economic fluctuations in time of crisis, the articulation of large firms to small firms to agricultural labour absorbs the oscillations.[19]

The subcontracting system has also remained important in particular regions and within given industries in other metropolitan countries. In West Germany, for instance, AEG, Krupp and Siemens were each reckoned to dominate between 20,000 and 30,000 small firms in 1965. In Italy a similar relationship has long existed in the metal processing industries of Emilia-Romagna, where artisan and small enterprise was still employing half of the industry's workforce in the late sixties. Studies have shown that in the overwhelming majority of cases these units survive as a result of conscious policy on the part of the large corporations. Perhaps even more significantly there is also evidence to suggest that such decentralisation of production on the Japanese model has in fact grown in several areas of the Italian centre and north, as larger enterprises have struggled to cut costs in the face of recent recessions.[20]

In Britain the structure of the heavily industrialised Midlands is still sharply divided between big capital and a myriad of small sub-contracting firms in the heavy engineering, machine tool and car manufacture sectors. Some fierce struggles took place in the seventies as black workers in particular fought to improve conditions in the many foundries, small engineering works and component plants that act as suppliers to the major vehicle manufacturers.

Sub-contractors and independent producers using antiquated technology need to exploit an unorganised workforce to survive. Conceding higher wages undermines their usefulness to larger firms and threatens to undermine their market position. They are highly vulnerable to imports from low-wage economies and, as microprocessors bring nearer the possibility of automating small-scale batch production, will increasingly need higher levels of fixed capital investment.

In short, local economies rebuilt around small manufacturing and processing enterprises will be low wage ones which are far from stable. And the extent to which any significant growth can occur will probably be dependent, as Tories like Howe have realised, not only on rate rebates and a loosening of planning controls, but also on an erosion of employment protection and health and safety legislation, in order to allow entrepreneurs to take maximum advantage of the oversupply of labour in the older urban areas.

In Hackney, average cash wages in the clothing trades declined by 16 per cent between December 1979 and August 1980—roughly a 30 per cent cut when inflation is taken into account.[21] If unemployment grows to a level where it has a fairly major and lasting impact on wage levels in the unorganised sectors, and it is politically possible to encode in law the divisions between different groups in the working class by attaching very different rights to employment in different size firms, then it may well become economically viable for British capital to pursue dual economy type arrangements on a much wider scale.

Office employment and the 'growth services'

Until the mid-sixties the decline of employment in London manufacturing was more than balanced by job creation in the fast expanding 'growth services'. The most important constituents of this division of the economy are insurance, banking, professional, scientific and business services, and public sector employment at both central and local government levels. Since 1966 the total number of jobs in these branches has continued to grow—but the rate of increase has been half of that elsewhere in the country and the expansion has failed to offset the decline in the other divisions. Furthermore, large numbers of London's already existing 'growth service' jobs are likely to be rationalised away in the coming decade, as public spending cuts hit state employment and recession forces the pace of restructuring in the private sector. Particularly important in this context is the coming technological transformation of office work, which—according to GLC esti-mates—will account for 40.3 per cent of all jobs in Greater London in 1981.[22]

The growth services account for a significantly higher proportion of total employment in London than in the other major conurbations. This spatial concentration reflects London's role as the centre of national government and the long period over which the City has functioned first as the undisputed hub of the world capital market and later as one of the major citadels of international finance capital. The expansion of office and growth service employment reflects a number of interrelated trends central to the post-war transformation of the capitalist system, including the proliferation of the state's functions; the continuing concentration and centralisation of capital leading to the forma-tion of multi-divisional concerns, increasingly transnational in operation; and the nature of the international division of labour, within which functions of control and administration are centralised in the major urban centres of the metropolitan nations.

By the end of the second world war the emphasis of economic activity in the City of London had already shifted from the physical exchange of goods and services to the exchange of rights and titles to goods and services as banking and stock exchange activities took up the available space. In the thirties the industrial companies setting up London head offices had begun to look to sites in and around the West End and, such was the demand for new offices, that—when controls were removed in 1954—rapid development of new offices followed. In the late fifties over 3.5 million sq. ft. was annually added to the London stock—giant blocks spilled over on to the South Bank, outdated buildings in the central districts were torn down and replaced, and speculators turned their attentions to working class streets north of the West End where land and profits could be picked up cheap. It looked like progress—it reminded people of New York.

Inside these 'office factories' large numbers of professional, management and supervisory jobs were coming into existence at the top end of the hierarchy—lower down an army of clerical and secretarial labour was being recruited. Office work had been an important source of employment for women in London since the turn of the century when the spread of the typewriter and tele-phone led employers to draw on the pool of educated female labour that secondary education had created. With post-war expansion the possibility of avoiding the factory and the shop by going into office work was now within reach of more and more working class women leaving school in the inner city and suburbs.

By the sixties however the state had come to see the concentration of new office work and development in the central business districts as a problem. The 'rush hour' was threatening to clog up the urban infrastructure, property speculators were giving free enterprise a bad name, and the concentration of rapidly growing office work in the South-East was being seen to undermine regional development policy. The response included setting up a bureau to encourage the private sector to decentralise office work from London, the formulation of plans to disperse some civil service departments to other cities, and the introduction of an Office Development Permit system in 1965, following a ban on new office building in London and its surrounding region imposed by the incoming Labour government the previous year. Operated tightly for the first couple of years, extended to cover other regions, then cut back to cover London and the South-East, the ODP system had some perverse effects. Its introduction coincided with the beginning of a period in which expansion of the state bureaucracy, mergers at home and incoming transnationals generated a high demand for London office space and, to the delight of the developers, rents rocketed. Between 1965 and the end of 1970—when the permit system had already been liberalised to the point of non-existence—the rental values of modern offices erected since the war increased by 380 per cent.[23]

While the ODP system is now viewed by politicians and planners as a failure, the activities of the Location of Offices Bureau (which before being abolished by the Tories in 1979 claimed responsibility for encouraging the decentralisation of 134,000 office jobs from Central London between 1963-76) are generally regarded as having been successful. (So successful in fact that cancellation of its original brief formed part of the 1976 policy package designed to stem inner city job loss.) The impact of the LOB's educational activities, though, needs to be put in perspective. For just as industrial dispersal policies coincided with a shift in the locational requirements of manufacturers, the policy of moving office jobs out coincided with developments that were in any case maturing in the sector as a result of market forces quite outside state control.

By the late sixties the costs of maintaining central London offices were rising sharply. Soaring rentals and rates were one factor—another was a mounting wages bill, reflecting allowances for commuting paid to top staff grades and periodic shortages of clerical and secretarial labour. The solution for employers was to decentralise in search of cheaper premises and a more disciplined workforce to carry out repetitive tasks, leaving behind a much smaller establishment of elite decision-takers and policy-makers, plus supporting staffs, who needed face to face contact with the world of business and government.

In the outer boroughs, office centres like Croydon had already grown considerably by this time and they continued to expand—but now firms which wanted to decentralise looked more and more beyond London's boundaries to towns like Reading, Southend, Sevenoaks and Tunbridge Wells. All but 24 per cent of the jobs relocated via the LOB between 1973-76 went to destinations in the South-East region—only 4 per cent of the total went to Inner London, 31 per cent went to Outer London, and 41 per cent to destinations in the rest of the South-East. The bureau's case studies of decentralised firms make interesting reading:

> Even though unemployment figures for office workers, at least in the South-East, will reveal very few unemployed office workers, once an office moves to a town it finds a very large hidden supply of potential labour, consisting largely of married women. These are often anxious to work but need to work near home because of family commitments. Most firms found their advertisements for vacancies vastly oversubscribed and therefore were able to choose the most suitable applicants. These married women are grateful for the opportunity to work locally and thus become loyal and hardworking employees: the older the employee the more reliable and responsible he [sic] is likely to be.[24]

In the actual move the common pattern is for routine staff to be made redundant—which explains why clerical workers have in fact figured prominently in the catalogue of inner city unemployment over the last ten years. At the other end senior staff continue to get the London rate, but routine office workers get lower wages—adding to the savings from lower rates of absenteeism and turnover and cheaper rents and local taxes.

Changes in the level and distribution of office employment in London reflect the growing importance of decentralisation with its attendant hiving off of labour-intensive functions to outer or out of London locations. In the ten years from 1966 the number of office workers employed in Central London fell from 754,000 to 680,000; at the same time the ratio of administrative and professional to clerical and secretarial workers rose.[25] Office employment in Outer London has been growing, but not at a fast enough rate to offset the decline in Inner and Central London—in the latter area the number of clerical and secretarial staff fell by 12.2 per cent in the decade to 1971, and the 1981 census will probably reveal that a similar rate of decline has held in both the central and inner areas throughout the seventies. It is already clear that many of the Inner London office centres designated in the Greater London Development Plan have failed to take-off—Brixton's 900,000 sq. ft. of new offices for example were never built, and the one large block that was completed remained untenanted for three years. The simple explanation is that inner areas cannot provide the combination of cheaper rents and a more docile labour force that the private sector is seeking out.

Nevertheless, office work remains an important source of employment for Londoners, accounting for 1.5 million jobs of which 60 per cent are in the clerical and secretarial grades. Nearly all of these are filled by residents of the conurbation. But it is no exaggeration to say that many of these jobs are now highly vulnerable . . . for the sector is already being hit by the beginnings of a transformation every bit as fundamental as anything that has happened in manufacturing since the second world war.

In their simplest form, 'wordprocessors' are electric typewriters with the addition of a memory. These allow the typist to correct and edit work without retyping the unaffected passages of text and are capable of automatically reproducing a large variety of standardised letters and documents, leaving only the variable details to be filled in. In more sophisticated systems the keyboard and 'visual display unit' are hooked into a mainframe computer and centralised electronic filing system. Documents are displayed and edited on screen and final copies are reproduced on very rapid printers. Once enough office 'work stations' are in operation documents can be routed over telephone lines to be printed out, if necessary, in the receiving offices. If paper versions of the communication are not required copies can be stored electronically by both sender and receiver. In this set up the worker, almost always a woman, is expected to perform continuously without ever needing to leave her seat for the filing cabinet or stationary cupboard and the management—as never before—has an effective way of constantly controlling her rate of work and measuring her productivity. Logica, the systems consultancy firm, claim that one typist on a wordprocessor can do the work of three and a half to five on conventional electric typewriters. For management, the benefits are clear—in the transfer to the electronic office not only secretarial but clerical staff can be shed. The remaining workers, however, will be faced with a highly controlled regime and the prospect of transfer to piecework methods of payment, a shift system that takes in the evenings (because of the advantages of constantly operating capital-intensive equipment) and new health and safety risks (from constant work in darkened rooms).[26]

West Germany is at present the major European market for the new technology and Siemens, a leading manufacturer, have estimated that 40 per cent of current office work will be automated by 1990. In France a recent government report on 'the computerisation of society' endorsed a forecast that the banking sector will shed 30 per cent of its staff in the next ten years. In Britain the rate of adoption has so far been slow—with some 9,000 systems installed as of June 1978 as against 45,000 in West Germany. But there are clear signs that the rate is increasing and ASTMS forecast that 2.6 million 'information workers' jobs will be lost by 1985 and that this will have risen to 3.9 million by 1991. For the state the advent of office mechanisation represents a major breakthrough—for, as O'Connor has stressed, the long-run failure to raise the productivity of administrative labour has been a major factor in precipitating the 'fiscal crisis of the state'.[27] Sustained public expenditure cuts are likely to significantly spur on the adoption of wordprocessors in the state bureaucracy.

For the 24 per cent of London's workforce employed in clerical/secretarial grades these trends have obvious implications. London's erstwhile 'growth services' embrace a high proportion of precisely those institutions and enterprises where the rate of adoption of the new technology will be comparatively swift. In the next decade this will compound the job loss already occurring as labour intensive functions are decentralised from the Central and Inner London areas. Given the fact that two-thirds of office workers are female—and nearly all women office workers are employed in the lower grades—the spread of wordprocessing is going to have its most traumatic impact on womens' employment.

For many women leaving school in the inner city, office employment has up to now been an escape route from the factory, the shop and the council estate—it has provided opportunities for job switching, picking up relatively well-paid temporary work, 'social mobility', and contact with other women.[28] But the coming electronic office will have a rising ratio of male administrators and professionals on its books—and female posts will be disproportionately filled by women from upper class backgrounds. The larger number of routine jobs—which will be deskilled even as they are drastically reduced in number—have traditionally gone to women of working class origin. They and their younger sisters are now likely to be confronted with an urban labour market which, as institutionalised sexism still holds sway, will force them back on to the estate and into the family in increasing numbers. In the next decade the decline of office employment will almost certainly be as important in the lives of the urban working class as the erosion of manufacturing employment has been in the last two decades.

Service city

Today we can no longer point to the factories, workshops and ports as the sole sites of industry. Modern industry has stamped its mechanised feet across the countryside and the sea, usurped the social processes of entertainment, recreation and culture, and through the electronic media assaults the inner citadel of our minds with relentless insistence. In particular, the 'personal service industries' surround us. We use them when we have our hair cut, clothes cleaned, car serviced, hail a taxi, place a bet, get take-away food, dance at a disco, go to a film, out for a drink or take a day trip. We consume their products in our 'free time', slipping into them like clean clothes at the end of a day's work. That's the reason why it's difficult to place them in capital's firmament. But in essence these industries extract surplus value, sell commodities and make profits in the same way as General Motors or ICI. The prodigious growth of the numbers they employ, the generally lower pay and productivity of labour, and the opportunities they have offered to small capital have marked the personal services out from the traditional heartlands of capitalist industry during the last thirty years. In the most dynamic subsectors—such as those in the leisure, entertainment and tourism businesses—some small firms gained sufficient room at the outset to grow into giants in the premier league and large-scale organisation has increased as manufacturing giants have broadened their base by acquiring expanding service sector enterprises. Many subsectors, however, such as motor vehicle repairs, hairdressing and launderettes, have largely remained the preserve of small business.

As new patterns of social life began to solidify after the war, the volume and variety of the personal services ripened in the greenhouse of rising living standards. This new social order involved an unprecedented expansion of the state's activities into the lives, the very front rooms, of the working class. It was a social order embracing changed family structures as well, and which both shaped and was shaped by the incorporation of many family and community activities into the market place. Here is how Braverman has described both the process leading to the 'consumer society' and its results:

> The social structure, built upon the market, is such that the relations between individuals and social groups do not take place directly, as co-operative human encounters, but through the market as relations of purchase and sale. Thus the more social life becomes a dense and close network of interlocked activities in which people are totally interdependent, the more atomised they become and the more contacts with one another separate them instead of bringing them closer . . . As the social and family life of the community are weakened, new branches of production are brought into being to fill the resulting gap; and as new services and commodities provide substitutes for human relations in the form of market relations, social and family life are further weakened. Thus it is a process that involves economic and social changes on the one side, and profound psychological and affective patterns on the other.[29]

The leading edge of these developments can be seen in the way that activities like computer dating, the marketing of sex and gambling have thrived ever more obviously off the atomisation of social life in the last decade.

London, like other great metropolitan cities, has a highly developed service sector. This facet of its economy is a reflection of its longstanding role as national capital. Even before the industrial revolution and Britain's rise to world economic power its concentration of aristocratic and merchant society made it the richest and largest consumer market in Europe; thereafter enormous population growth paralleled the expansion of the Empire; and throughout the present century it has retained its role both as an international city and the hub of Britain's richest region. The last two decades, however, have seen rapid population dispersal and a decline in the average Londoner's income vis-à-vis the national average and the growth points of employment in the personal service sector are now highly dependent on the continued and very uncertain expansion of tourism. Retailing shows the trends evident throughout the personal service sector.

London remains the largest shopping centre in the country's most prosperous region—but its lead has been slipping. In 1961 London sales accounted for 55 per cent of regional turnover, but by the time of the 1971 census of distribution this had fallen to 50 per cent and the available evidence suggests this trend has continued. It is hardly a surprising one given that rapid population dispersal has operated largely through the private house buying market and so favoured higher income households. Within London the centre's domination over the rest of the capital was in fact increasing during the sixties—the district inside the main railway termini increased its share of turnover in the conurbation from 17 per cent to 20 per cent in the ten years to 1971. But over the seventies the flow of day-trip shoppers from the rest of the region fell as transport costs rose and decentralisation of investment brought the famous name stores nearer to the home counties middle class. Offsetting this in the mid and late seventies was a boom in retail sales to tourists—largely contingent on the decline of the pound which for a short while made the UK the bargain basement of Europe. This was a godsend for Oxford Street which took £250 million of the £750 million foreign tourists spent in British shops during 1977.

In the inner boroughs, where most of the city's retail workers actually live, the story was already very different. Brixton, for example, was the pre-eminent South London shopping centre from the end of the last century until the fifties. By the beginning of the sixties, however, some signs of decline were evident—even though it was still only rivalled by the outer London centres of Kingston to the west and Croydon to the south.

The borough council spent the next five years planning a strategy whereby public spending on transport and housing would act as a catalyst for massive private sector investment in offices and modern shops, and the combination of the two would reverse the process of decline. Its 1967 master plan provided for clearance and redevelopment of 84 'prime site acres'; the construction of a five level transport interchange embracing the ill-fated inner ringway motorway, the BR suburban railway, pedestrian walkways and the new Victoria line underground; up to 900,000 sq. ft. of new offices; a series of new shopping plazas; ten of the tallest residential towerblocks in Europe; cinemas, a health centre, a library, a sports centre and a new square with a lake which would be artificially frozen over for ice skating! But local opposition to the tower blocks, rivalry between property companies trying to extract better terms from the council, uncertainty about the expansion plans of major traders and the imminent axing of the motorway box system all combined to hold up the beginning stages of this fairytale transformation of one of London's ghetto areas.

As late as 1973 Ravenseft developers were still pushing for plans that included 450,000 sq. ft. of new shop space, but with the collapse of the property boom they withdrew. By 1976 a consultant's report had concluded that there was no prospect of attracting private investment and that no new shops would be built because, far from there being a clear and rising market demand, there was a considerable doubt about Brixton's future as a shopping centre because of declining local income. Since then the decline has continued with the majority of major traders either pulling out or failing to make the investments that, a decade before, had been judged essential parts of reversing the process. Thus one of the earliest attempts to harness private capital to the cause of inner city regeneration has failed even as these same groups have been investing heavily in such projects as the new £39 million shopping complex at Milton Keynes.

Retailing's growing dependence on tourism was mirrored right across London's service industries during the seventies. The number of foreign visitors to the UK rose from 1 million in 1959 to 11.5 million in 1978, when tourism was Britain's top foreign currency earner, accounting for over half the country's 'invisible exports'. Together with internal tourism it directly or indirectly sustains 1.5 million jobs—over 500,000 in London. By 1976 it was estimated that foreign tourists were spending nearly a billion pounds in the capital, making a tenth of all journeys on the underground, accounting for 40 per cent of theatre takings, and providing the main market for numerous leisure enterprises as well as the hotel and catering industries. During the following two years extravagant projections of future growth were common-place—but since 1979 the strength of sterling, the weakness of the dollar and renewed recession and inflation have combined to hit the industry hard. In addition visitors are spending fewer nights in the capital—and as a result tourist spending in the city is estimated to have fallen by between 20 per cent and 30 per cent between 1978 and 1980.[30]

The ability to draw on an unorganised workforce is very important for both big and small companies in the labour-intensive hotel, catering industries and other service activities, where the wages bill is high in relation to turnover and annual, seasonal, and daily peaks and troughs in demand are inherent in the business. In this situation groups like Trust House Forte and Garners are prepared to fight long and hard to retain the casual labour system and unilateral control over the labour process. This and the considerable problems facing activists seeking to organise in the sector have insured that union membership has remained as low as 3 per cent. With low wages and appalling conditions the norm rather than the exception, employers are prepared to tolerate a high turnover of labour, looking to migrant and immigrant workers of both sexes and indigenous women workers to fill the vacancies. Recruitment abroad has been a standard feature of many chains' policies for twenty years—in 1971 40 per cent of London's hotel workers and 50 per cent of restaurant workers were immigrants or migrants. Traditionally these workers have been used to fill the worst jobs which local workers resist taking—and this explains why the employers have generally resisted attempts to reduce the number of work permits issued to incoming workers. Recently, however, there have been signs that this situation has changed—as a representative from Grand Metropolitan Hotels has said: 'We no longer need to bring in workers from abroad because we can find sufficient labour from deprived urban communities.'[31]

The build up of the surplus population in London and the conurbations

London stands at one end of the spectrum of British conurbations. It is marked out by its enormous size, by its situation at the centre of the prosperous South-East and by peculiarities of class structure stemming from the concentration of 'growth service' sectors within its bounds. Nevertheless, despite its privileged position as world city and pivot of the national economy, there are clear signs that its urban economy is slipping into deep trouble.

As manufacturing employment has been cut in half over the last twenty years, relatively archaic forms of production have come to make up a greater proportion of what remains. And as suburbanisation and population dispersal have proceeded, there has been a shift in emphasis within the wider service economy away from activities related to the vitality of the productive infrastructure and the wealth of the resident population as a whole, towards services revolving around tourism and the luxury expenditure of the resident rich. In the course of these developments many skilled and/or well paid jobs have disappeared and low productivity labour-intensive activities have increased as a proportion of the whole. This shift is perceivable in individual histories such as those of the ex-dockers who now work on pleasure boats, or those of women now taking menial jobs they would previously have avoided—perhaps at a time when their husbands had better paid more skilled work, or they themselves had a manufacturing job. It is a shift carved into the structure of the city in places like St Katherine's dock—once an important part of the import/export infrastructure, now a hotel/marina complex—and one also reflected in trends concerning wages and household incomes.

In cash terms London wages continue to be higher on average than elsewhere, but the differential has been narrowing and for manual workers it definitely does not offset the higher cost of living in London (estimated to be 14 per cent above the national average in the mid-seventies, largely as a result of housing and transport costs which have both risen sharply since). Between 1975 and 1978 the average earnings of men over 19 in manual jobs in London declined from 107.5 per cent to 104 per cent of the national average—over the same period the average earnings of women in manual jobs declined from 115 per cent to 110 per cent of the national average for workers so described. Household incomes exhibit similar trends with London's poor getting poorer both in relation to the better off layers of the city's society and in relation to the poor in the country as a whole. The Family Expenditure Survey reports show that between 1970 and 1975 the average income (wages plus benefits) of the poorest 25 per cent of London's households declined from 65.4 per cent of the national median to 53.2 per cent, while the average income of the poorest 25 per cent of households nationally was declining from 60.1 per cent to 54.4 per cent of the median.[32]

In the light of the structural trends we have analysed and the national/international economic situation, the outlook for London in the eighties looks bad. Closures since the onset of the 1980 recession have shown that the contraction of manufacturing has far from run its course. With national output expected to be up to 20 per cent below its 1979 level in 1982, a further significant drop in employment in this sector of the capital's economy is almost certainly imminent. Outside this sector, erstwhile 'growth services' are themselves shedding labour—decentralisation and technological innovation are affecting both public and private office employment, and cuts in state expenditure are beginning to bite at both central and local government level, tourism is in trouble. All these factors point to a substantial rise in unemployment which is already at a historically high level.

The official unemployment rate figures for London published by central government are misleading. They express the number of unemployed as a percentage of all those employed and unemployed in the conurbation, and by including nearly 500,000 commuters in the employed total push down the figure for Londoners out of work. To get a more accurate picture one has to turn to the residential male unemployment figures produced by the GLC. (Figures and percentages for women out of work are so misleading as to not be worth using, even on a residential basis, because so much female unemployment goes unrecorded. The mass of women seeking work are not eligible for benefits either because in the past they have not paid full insurance contributions or because they are the dependants of male wage earners and thus cannot collect unemployment money from social security. The General Household Survey in 1976 found that 54 per cent of women who described themselves as seeking work were not registered as unemployed as opposed to 7.5 per cent of men.)

Table 5: Resident Male Unemployment Rates

April of each year—in percentages

	1971	1972	1973	1974	1975	1976	1977	1978	1979	July 1980
London	2.7	3.2	2.5	2.3	3.3	5.4	5.0	5.4	4.9	5.5
Inner NE	3.8	4.7	3.6	3.3	4.6	7.4	7.8	7.7	7.1	8.6
Inner S	3.7	4.2	3.2	3.1	4.4	6.8	7.1	6.9	6.1	6.5
Inner NW	3.2	3.7	2.9	2.6	4.1	7.0	8.1	8.0	6.6	7.4
Inner London	3.6	4.3	3.3	3.0	4.4	7.1	7.6	7.5	6.6	7.5
Outer London	1.9	2.4	1.8	1.6	2.4	3.9	3.9	3.8	3.4	3.9
Rest of South East	2.4	2.7	1.9	1.9	2.9	4.1	4.3	4.0	3.5	4.0
GB	3.7	4.7	3.5	3.3	4.5	5.9	6.0	6.0	5.6	6.5

Source: Information provided by GLC Policy and Intelligence Branch.

Table 5 shows that unemployment grew rapidly in line with the national trend throughout the seventies. But the figures also show that the overall male unemployment rate—although markedly higher than that in the surrounding region—has continued to run well below the national rate. Within London, however, there are areas of much higher unemployment and there is a significant differential between the inner and outer areas—in contrast to the inner areas the outer ones in fact have a male unemployment rate below that for the rest of the South-East. What is striking about the rate for the inner areas is that, while in the early seventies it too was running below the national average, in 1976 the position was reversed (compare lines 5 and 8 of the table), and since then Inner London has had a level of unemployment considerably above that of the country as a whole. In April 1979 fifteen out of the twenty exchange areas in the inner areas had a significantly higher rate than the national average and three of them one that was more than double the national average of 5.6 per cent.[33] In April 1976 male unemployment in Poplar was running at 15 per cent and in Stepney at 13.4 per cent—three years later it had declined marginally to 13.8 per cent and 13.3 per cent respectively. But what has been noticeable is that in these inner areas and others like them unemployment has been slow to respond to the hesitant and uneven recovery that characterised the labour market nationally during 1978-79. (The same was true after the previous low point in late 1973).

In gauging the real level of unemployment one also needs to bear in mind categories that do not figure in the official statistics even when these are presented on a residential basis. There are those who are currently kept off the register through temporary schemes in localities of already high unemployment and also a group of people, mainly young, who do not register, either because the minimum to which they are entitled is so little and/or because they wish to avoid the attentions of the Unemployment Review Officer whose job it is to force them into taking dead-end jobs. This is especially true for young West Indians—although they figure prominently among the registered unemployed, a succession of surveys has revealed that anything up to 60 per cent are not claiming in some areas. A local employment exchange official estimated that as of mid-1979 there were two to three thousand unregistered unemployed young West Indians in the Brixton area of London alone.[34] Taking these excluded categories and a detailed estimate for women's unemployment into account the Liverpool City Planning Officer calculated the real rate of city-wide unemployment to be running at 22 per cent in January 1980, (at a time when the Department of Employment statistic for unemployment in the 'travel to work area' was 12.7 per cent), and that the two inner city planning districts had unemployment rates of 37 per cent and 31 per cent respectively.[35]

The build-up of unemployment in major urban areas is an important indicator of the relative concentration of the growing 'surplus population' in the conurbations. The vast majority of people unemployed in these areas fall within the broad definition of the surplus population that we have adopted. However, as we stressed in the Introduction, the surplus population is not just another term for the unemployed, nor for that matter 'the lumpenproletariat' or 'the reserve army of labour'. Groups other than the unemployed are part of the surplus population and we will be looking at questions concerning the family and household structure which impinge on this problem in the next chapter. Equally, when we use the term surplus population we are not simply referring to people who lack an inside toilet, who live in a decaying environment or—in the words of the White Paper on the Inner Cities—suffer from a sense of 'collective deprivation'. What we are doing is talking about the concentration in the major urban areas of people who stand in a particular relationship to the capitalist economy and the capitalist state—a relationship that is primarily economic but has important political ramifications.

To recap, these groups include all those who are long-term unemployed; most of those for whom periods of unemployment alternate with dependence on temporary or casual part-time work; those participating in the bottom reaches of the 'black economy' outside the tax system; all those who are totally dependent on state benefits or forms of charity (including the mass of pensioners, the chronically sick and disabled, and single parent families on social security); and those people who, although in regular employment in labour-intensive sweated occupations or the state service sector, earn wages significantly below the national average and who live in households where the standard of living only exceeds the minimum poverty level because of the receipt of means-tested benefits. This broad definition embraces the majority of those living in urban areas who are unemployed because they are marginal to the requirements of capital in terms of the direct production of surplus value during the current long wave of stagnation, but does not draw a hard and fast distinction between them and the low-paid who are in work or those who are excluded from the workforce because of age and childcare responsibilities—because in practice the line is often crossed by individual people.

When these groups are considered together it is clear that in some areas of the big cities we are talking about a surplus population of very considerable proportions: in the case of Liverpool for example, it probably approaches half the adult population on a city-wide basis and exceeds this level in the inner areas.

The proportions of the surplus population today cannot be calculated from the 1971 census—nor can the breaches that divide groups in the surplus population from the rest of the working class be nailed down by studies using the commonly accepted social class categories corresponding to a thoroughly inappropriate nineteenth century division of labour. It is a political category rather than a sociological one, and one which we have adopted because it allows us to approach divides within the working class that are assuming urgent significance.

As for London, we can learn something from its history. It may be at one end of the spectrum of conurbations today, but it is also the only major British city to have undergone a comparable process of deindustrialisation before—and a consequent major expansion of the surplus population within its bounds. How this happened during the middle decades of the last century has been instructively analysed by Gareth Steadman Jones in his book *Outcast London*.[36] It was a time when the upswing of industrialisation had the effect of decimating major London manufacturing industries and the contradictions of capitalist urban development resulted in a significant proportion of the city's population becoming marginalised. In the years of the Great Depression that followed the state was faced with new and massive problems of public order. There then existed possibilities of creating powerful alliances between certain layers in the more prosperous organised working class and groups in the surplus population.[37] In the event, the forms of organisation that were created failed to heal the divides and create more than transitory unities. Today—a century later, living through another long wave of stagnation—approaching similar problems has become an urgent task. However, we would argue that unity can only be built on the basis of a politics that addresses the needs of those groups, who, divided from each other, are united in their alienation from labourism. In the next two chapters—which focus on the family, and the relationship of the state's repressive apparatus to the surplus population—we look at the experience of these groups in greater detail before drawing out the political implications of this analysis.

5. The Fragmented Family

When I saw it first, because water was under the stairs, I went back to the Town Hall and told them I didn't want it. And they said to me they had nothing more to offer me. I might have to wait for six months . . . I was in the valley of decision, I didn't know what to do, but since I've been here, I suffer in all departments . . . The windows are so draughty I can't light a lamp. It's dark in here now and there's no light coming from the window with the big wall over there. You can imagine when it's night and the curtain is closed, it's like a prison cell . . . Sometimes I can't sleep at night because four of us sleep in the bed. And when my boy isn't well I have to sit up every night with him. Sometimes I have to sleep in hospital with him, he spent the whole month of May in hospital last year. Now he's going to a special school and he can't keep up with it . . . he can't sleep at night when he's wheezing. He's going down, going down. He can't go out to play, even if he's feeling well . . . I'm trying my best with the children. But then they won't be with me in this condition. They will get fed up, maybe start drifting away. My eldest boy I want him to stay on at school, but he says if I'm living in this condition it's not encouraging to stay on in school, because he can't even study. He wants to leave school this summer. He was going to stay on, but seeing as we can't get out of here, he lost confidence . . . I've tried my best, I knock at every door, I can't get any help. They just don't want to know anyone in Wynn House . . . I can't get HP. That television is lent to me by my friend from the church. We have no milkman coming in here, so we are shut off; we are in a world of our own . . . You know sometimes I just feel I could walk out and leave them, that's just how I feel. Then I have to think again. I walk out and leave him, he's going to get worse, because he can't do without me. That's what's holding me back in this place. It's like serving a life sentence in this place; you don't know when it will stop. I'm serving a life sentence for a crime I haven't committed.

So speaks a West Indian woman, a parent and a single mother. She is one of a growing army of women in the inner city who are raising children on their own.

Family life seems to be buckling, cracking at some points, as its structures shift into line with present day realities and it's in the inner city districts that the dissolution of blood and marriage ties has reached its height. In some London boroughs one in three of all families are now headed by a lone parent. Every year in the inner city more and more old people find themselves living alone as their children move away and family networks break down. The cyclone of social change that has enveloped the old working class areas has ripped its way through the old family structures and flung out atomised individuals. As this has happened pundits and politicians have come to hark ever more noticeably on the critical state of the family. And when the storm has passed the individuals still confront a life in which class, sex and race define the possibilities.

At one end of the spectrum young white professionals who separate from their spouses can find a new flat in the suburbs or in a smart central district. If lonely they can frequent a single's wine bar, try computer dating, a holiday romance or the lonely hearts columns. At the other end: a drab damp flat on a dump estate, the remorseless struggle to survive on social security, the enforced isolation when there's no one to babysit, the weight of sole responsibility for the kids, the doctor's tranquillisers . . .

To look for the family in the city is to enter a hall of mirrors. Each panel displays a facet of this universe of the family: the self-contained suburban units, the hostels full of Scots and Irish migrants, the squatted communes, the old people alone, the dump estates, fourth girl wanted for Victoria flat. It is not easy to observe the shifting reflections of anger, pain and frustration. No one lives outside these conflicts—to witness them is also to experience their internal echoes. Nor is it easy to grasp the great diversity of family life in the city without losing sight of common patterns beneath the confusion.

Looking back to the birth of industrial capitalism, it is possible to pick up the trail of the family and trace in outline its development up to modern times. Before industrialisation, the family was frequently an economic unit and the family home was often the place of work for the whole family. With the burgeoning of industrial capitalism, however, production inside the home —whether for family consumption or for the market—declined, while that outside the home expanded greatly. The uncontrolled excesses of capital's first flush of accumulation, accompanied as they were by the vast migration from country to town, brought havoc to the family. There followed tumultuous decades during which one of the principal aims of much working class agitation was the preservation of traditional economic relationships within the family.[1] Contemporary accounts provide some record of the repercussions of migration and economic change on family life when they describe the hoardes of parentless children who survived in the central city 'rookeries' or slums; the canal-side encampments of migrant workers where marriage was forgotten; the occupants of the poorhouses and the agricultural gang labourers, who veered between city slum and the country at harvest time.

Out of this first phase of industrialisation a new family order came about. In the middle class residential suburbs of the towns and cities the family home now became a consciously created retreat from the harsh world of commerce—the wife's tasks in life being to bear children, supervise the servants and welcome the master home to his haven at the end of the day. Both church and state transmitted this vision of the family to the working class as part and parcel of their growing attempt to regulate working class sexual morality and social life. The skilled and better-off sections of the working class, where they were successful in their agitation for a wage sufficient to keep the wife at home, were in fact able to partially emulate the middle class model of family life. But for the vast majority of the working class, such a choice was not possible. Instead a new family structure began to emerge which reached out beyond the confines of one married couple, and in doing so bound together a large number of relatives into a web of mutual support and solidarity. It is this form of family structure which has been called the extended family.

> Children seem so restless somehow nowadays, always on the move.
> It didn't used to be like this . . . Five brothers I had and three
> sisters—I was the last but one, and we were all on steel and tinplate
> here in Morriston, sisters and husbands and all. And we all lived
> close, and went to the same chapel . . . Yes, that was the thing about
> us—we all lived close, perhaps too close I sometimes say when you
> think of the animosities and so on that cropped up now and then.
> But in those days you just had to help one another—there was no
> welfare state then. When all the men were out at the works there'd
> be no money coming in from anywhere. That's when you needed
> the family and good neighbours. We were all in the same boat
> together. All the men of the family, uncles, cousins and all, would
> go picking coal together up on the tips, or hunting rabbits.[2]

The memories of this old man from Swansea were recorded in the early 1960s. They formed part of a study of working class family life—one of many being done at that time—which give a vivid picture of the extended family just before it passed away. Young and Wilmott's study of Bethnal Green in East London—perhaps the most influential of these studies—revealed a close-knit community where most people had a relative, if not in the same street, then just around the corner. Here brothers, sisters, parents, children and grandparents saw each other frequently. The whole complex of blood relatives did not exclude friends and neighbours, but rather acted as a bridge integrating individuals into the solidarity of a wider working class community.

Binding this family network together was not just love or affection but a very real material exchange of services. Mothers were a fount of advice and knowledge to their daughters and looked after the grandchild when the daughter was ill, went out to work, had a night out, or just went shopping. In these communities, 'the daughter's labours [were] in a hundred little ways shared with the older woman whose days of child-bearing [but not of child-rearing] are over'. Old people in return could expect to be looked after in their old age, cared for as part of the family rather than ending their days in the workhouse or home. At the centre of this family and community structure was the mother-daughter relationship.

This close-knit working class community is often seen as a traditional way of life stretching back for centuries. Certainly the old man from Swansea saw it this way even though his own father was a migrant from the countryside in Victorian times. But there is little that is very traditional about it. Subsistence wages, the constant influx of migrants into the rapidly growing towns, appalling living conditions all worked against the widespread establishment of such a stable family and community structure for a long time. It was probably not until the 1880s that the extended family well and truly began to take root in the working class districts of the city. By then several generations were living in one place and the gradual rise in living standards, and then later the first state welfare measures, helped the process. A number of studies have persuasively argued that the provision of a state pension—the first was the non-contributory Lloyd George pension of 1906—was sufficient to take the edge off the extreme burden which fell on a family supporting its 'aged poor'.[3] This allowed genuinely affectionate and non-calculative support systems to grow up, although both the 1906 pension and the later 1928 contributory pension were not sufficient to make the old financially independant and most pensioners were partially supported by their families.

These early state interventions, unlike what was to follow, allowed working class communities to develop a culture and a solidarity which made the extended family a closed world to outsiders and agents of authority. However even in these years the extended family was never universal. It was always liable to disruption—particularly if the local economy underwent far reaching changes leading to internal or external migration. By the 1930s it was taking a battering in the declining industrial areas as young people flooded to the Midlands and South, leaving behind them the old, stranded without their children. The upheavals of the thirties, however, were only a foretaste of what was to come after the war. From then on the massive slum clearance programmes, the migration to new towns and suburbs, and a changing industrial structure and division of labour, all combined to thoroughly disrupt working class community and family life.

After the war, on the new estates and in the suburbs, a new prospect for family life was opening up—a modern house with running hot and cold water, an inside toilet, a clean and spacious environment for the kids, the promise of a garden, new schools—a fresh start in life away from the grime, the overcrowding of tenements in the old areas. It was alluring, but there was a price to pay: the new house would be more expensive, there were no corner shops or local pubs, and other members of the family would be at the end of a long and costly journey rather than just round the corner. Working class families were posed with a sharp choice between decent housing in a good environment without friends and family, and a crumbling flat in Bethnal Green near all that was dear to them. But despite attachments and misgivings many did go and there was no stopping the general drift from the old working class districts. As working class families moved out to these new suburban estates their structure tended to adopt the nuclear form. This happened at the very time that the whole complex of social change brought about during the course of the boom was beginning to undermine the stability of the nuclear family by heightening the contradictions at its heart.

The state has long recognised (as socialists have more recently) the crucial role of the family in serving to stabilise and reproduce capitalist social relations. Perhaps at the centre of this capacity is the way the family acts as a counterbalance to the inhumanity, the boredom and the alienation of social relations surrounding work.[4] Men experience this aspect of the family in quite different ways to women; for the working men of Ashton, a coal-mining village in Yorkshire, the family home is:

> a place where they can enjoy privacy if they ever feel the need of it, and, very important, a haven for the tired man when he returns

from work; here he expects to find a meal prepared, a room clean and tidy, a seat comfortable and warm, and a wife ready to give him what he wants.

But for a woman this structure has very different meanings: it involves the suppression of her self, of her needs and the channelling of her energy into the fulfillment of the personal desires of others. The family may be a haven for the man, but for the woman it can be more like a cage. And yet with the dissolution of wider family and community relationships the family is the only place where men and women can find the love, sensitivity and comfort they need.

The flux of the last thirty years may have dented sexist attitudes somewhat, but it has also greatly increased the isolation experienced at home by most working class women. With men and women coming to the hearth from such different places, and it still being for both the sole repository of personal meaning, it is not surprising that family life can be such a fraught affair. As Sheila Rowbotham has put it:

> chased out of the dominant mode of production where there is no room for emotion, such characteristics as love, tenderness and compassion assume a mawkish guise from confinement. The family is thus in one sense a dummy ideal, the repository of ghostly substitutes, emotional fictions which dissolve into cloying sentimentality or explode into thrashing, battering remorseless violence.

While this contradiction has always been central to the patriarchal family under capitalism, the last fifty years of social change have kicked away many of the props that previously contained it. As we saw in Chapter 2, one of the major developments of the post-war period was the influx of women into waged labour. This has had important repercussions for the stability of the family. Whereas before the war, working class women tended—with some notable exceptions[5]—to give up paid work after they had children, in the post-war period, the tendency has been for working class women to return to waged labour after a brief period off when the children are born. In order to cope with the extra demands made on them through having to hold down two jobs, women have increasingly turned to the market for provision of services which were previously provided by their unwaged labour in the home. This trend has both facilitated and been reinforced by the growth of new service industries and the manufacture of labour-saving consumer durables.

Other influences too have been at work reshaping this most intimate capsule of contradictory meanings and emotions. The inter-war years put an end to the tendency for women of all classes to rear large numbers of children. Over the last fifty years the proportion of families with two children has in fact doubled, while the proportion with five children or more has decreased from nearly one third to under a tenth. The move to a smaller family size is closely related to the compression of fertility within the life cycle of women. Throughout the post-war period the tendency has been towards a smaller family which is reared in a shorter period.

Migration and this changing internal shape of the family has hit the extended family hard. There are fewer daughters to look after the old people, they are more likely to have moved away from their parents' home town and to have a job as well as their own children to look after. At the same time as these informal systems of solidarity have been swept away, the contradictions impinging on family life have been sharpened.

While motherhood has remained the ideologically constructed number one goal and role in life for women, 'maternity has become quantitatively less and less significant in womens lives', and easily available and fairly reliable contraception has made motherhood in part a choice. And while women are still 'defined primarily through our destinies as wives and mothers—to be somebody else's private life',[6] they have become an ever increasing and more vital part of the workforce, with the power of a wage to help them decide about their own private life should they so choose. With the changes that have led more and more women to plant their feet both on the office floor and in the kitchen the old order has experienced tremors in all departments—from the bedroom to the trade union branch meeting.

We can see many of these processes at work in a speeded up and highly visible form when we look at the impact of the journey to Britain on the Asian family. International migration and racist immigration laws have broken many extended families by separating relatives, but this is not the whole story. Even in cases where the whole family network has travelled to Britain, the alien society's ways have worked into the family, like salt crystals into a knee joint, creating conflict, scarring and separation. Amrit Wilson has described the Gujerati joint family's journey since its arrival in Britain:

The whole joint family is on the scene, bearing the onslaught of British society and groaning with agony as a result — groaning on the one hand because of the intense racism and poverty it faces and on the other because of the confusions caused by the irrelevance in Britain of its most valued concepts . . . The most important controlling factor in these families is not the male ego but hierarchy. However in Britain, with most adult members of the family earning a wage and with working life separate from family life, hierarchy becomes a very weak concept.

In the Indian subcontinent the elders of a joint family had real power both through control of the family's money and through the power invested in them by tradition. In Britain their economic power has gone and the tradition is not strong when the dominant culture does not respect it. Very bitter conflicts between the generations have erupted as the elders are thrown into utter confusion at their powerlessness. They respond with their age old weapons, by trying to order their daughters-in-law about, taking away their jewellery, making their lives impossible with hundreds of petty rules.[7]

For Asian women the sundering of old family ways is not necessarily retrogressive in the long-term. But for young Asian women breaking away involves a very stark choice — losing family and friends in a racist society or submitting to father and husband and so being isolated from the mainstream of society. Despite the desperate attempts of the elders to maintain the old order the consequences of the migration seem inexorable—'as for the Gujerati joint family, it looks as if nothing can save it now'.

The images of family life are all-pervasive; warm and cosy, a haven from the brutish impersonal world outside; a retreat where we have something no one can take away; a safe world filled with Mum and Dad, a bright young boy and a sweet little girl in quiet harmony around the fire. We all share these images—whether our own family fits them or not—for they have become part of our culture, to be played on remorselessly by the conductors of mass consciousness swirling their siren songs through our minds. And yet these images, at once so powerful, are so at odds with reality. At any one time three-quarters of all households in Britain contain no children at all, let alone happy TV children. After the relatively brief period of raising children, the family only exists for most adults at odd weekends and holidays. And nowhere is this sanctified vision of family life more at variance with life itself than in the inner city. In the inner city with its low pay and desperate housing conditions it is hardest for a working class couple to create a family home with the minimum of material comforts and security necessary for it to be any sort of haven. Here too are the greatest concentrations of single adults, single parent families, familyless migrant workers and old living alone.

The dissolution of extended family networks and the trend towards smaller family units has stranded large numbers of old people without family support. As the proportion of pensioners in the population has increased, more and more of them have had to face the situation of living alone.[8] A Nuffield study of 1947 found that 22 per cent of women over 80 were living alone. Thirty years on, Age Concern found that 40 per cent of women aged 75 and over were living alone. These national figures conceal local variations—it is the big cities that contain the greatest numbers of solitary old people. In Inner London in 1971 31 per cent of all persons of pensionable age were living alone as against 23 per cent in Outer London.

In the past living alone did not necessarily mean isolation and loneliness. On the contrary the Bethnal Green study concluded 'The great majority of old people in Bethnal Green thought they best served their own interests and those of their children by living near them rather than with them.'[9] At the time of the survey in the late fifties, 77 per cent of old people still had a child within five minutes walk despite the beginnings of external migration. It was in this situation that the reciprocal exchange of services could take place. Only one in twenty-five of those interviewed saw one of their children less than once a week. Contrast this with the late seventies, where an inner city survey showed the proportion of old people living within five minutes walk of one of their children was halved to 37 per cent.[10] And now it was one in three of the elderly—not one in twenty-five—who saw their children less than once a week.

As a result of the post-war transformation of the social landscape the hopes of the inner city elderly to live independently but close to their children have been frustrated. For many independence has come to mean isolation as their children have moved to a New Town or entered owner-occupation in the suburbs. Over a third of those living alone interviewed by Age Concern said they had never dreamed they could be as lonely as they now are. Those old people with sufficient savings often try to resolve the problem by either moving to the coastal retirement belt or moving close to their children. It is in fact the upper middle classes of the Home Counties who now find it easiest to reproduce the solution favoured by the old East Enders in the fifties.

The rise in the number of single person households is a major feature of the changing social landscape of the big cities. As families with children have left, not only have the old been stranded but young single people have flocked in, while older single people—unlike their married counterparts—have tended to stay where they are. By 1971 the number of single person households in London had grown by a third over the previous decade to account for a third of all the city households.

In order to get an estimate of the number of adults living outside the conventional family unit, we have to add to these single households the many single people who share accommodation and the vast majority of those in institutions who have either separated or never married. In addition there are the rapidly growing numbers of single parent families. In 1978 they accounted for over one in four of all families in seven Inner London boroughs (and for a similar proportion in Manchester and around one in six in Liverpool and Birmingham). Taken together, this means that the proportion of all *households* which do not conform to the male-headed nuclear family norm is now over half of all households in Inner London. It is difficult to translate these figures on households into actual numbers of people—but we would estimate that between a third and a half of all those living in Inner London now live outside male-headed nuclear families.

Between 1971 and 1976 the number of one parent families in the United Kingdom increased by a third to around 750,000 families with 1,250,000 children.[11] By 1980 the number had climbed to 920,000—one in eight families nationally. The bulk of this increase has been due to the rise in the number of broken marriages which has resulted in an estimated 111,000 divorced mothers with children over the five year period. The other large increase was in the number of unmarried mothers, up by 40,000. Single parent families, like the old living alone, are not evenly distributed throughout the country—of the 65 parliamentary constituencies in the 20 borough/districts with the highest proportion of lone parent families, 37 are in London and a further 18 are in the Liverpool and Manchester conurbations. A survey of lone parent families in London has also found that half have been there for ten years or more and a further fifth between five and ten years.[12] So it seems that this concentration is due less to the migration of such families into the inner areas and more to the fact that family breakdown is greatest here, as is the number of women who decide to have children without male support.

The inner city is a place where more and more adults are raising children outside the established structures of a nuclear family. Lone fathers are more likely to keep the family home and to be financially secure after a marriage breakdown[13]—and as a result the problems of poverty and homelessness faced by single mothers are usually more acute than those faced by single fathers. The complex of problems facing women alone with kids also differs according to class and colour. A white professional mother separating from her husband is undoubtedly going to have a hard struggle to look after her children and continue working—but that struggle is more likely to take place in a decent home with a garden and on an income which permits holidays and the use of a car. At the other extreme is the situation which faces a very large number of single women with children—a situation graphically described to us by women who repeatedly and independently compared the experience of living their lives on inner urban estates to serving a prison sentence.

When family break-up involves loss of housing single parents usually find themselves in the waiting rooms of a local authority homeless families unit. It is usually the beginning of long grey months full of hints, warnings, delays and offers of semi-derelict property: the adult alone with kids has been classified as the head of a 'problem family' who—in the eyes of the housing bureaucracy—has the makings of a bad tenant likely to get into arrears and whose children are unlikely to fit into a 'nice estate'.

Through the classification systems of housing visitors, the policies of housing departments, and through the process of becoming homeless, a relative concentration of working class single parent families housed on council 'dump estates' has occurred. Although the problems of single parent families living in bad conditions are acute in a range of housing situations, surveys done on council house lettings in London have confirmed that on unmodernised inter-war or pre-first world war estates there are very high proportions of single parent families.[14] Many such estates are made up exclusively of these families along with black and immigrant worker families. This is in sharp contrast to the lettings on the more desirable modernised estates or the cottage type estates in Outer London where the units have been let almost exclusively to white, male-headed nuclear families.

In their routine processing of housing applications and in their housing policies, many local authorities reinforce the divisions which already exist inside the working class. In doing this the relative privileges of those white working class families who gain access to better quality public housing are confirmed, and the awful conditions of life of the rest are used as a justification for keeping them where they are; for the popular myths assert that the inhabitants of a dump estate are responsible for the conditions on it. In these ways the people in greatest need of good accommodation, because of the problems of bringing up children alone, actually end up concentrated in the worst public housing. Blame the victim is the name of the game, and welfare state managers are keen players.

* * *

From the road Wynn House has a long face and small windows; tucked in close to the prison, it used to house the screws. Inside the stained tarmac courtyard the block looms forbiddingly, although it is only five stories high. It is dark here even in summer, the brickwork blackened, the sky small. The horizon just one hundred yards away. The wind turns the corner, whipping up old paper from the yard, looking for an exit. On one side of the courtyard, next to the rubbish containers, empty milk crates provide the children's only playground. Starting from a wet basement level the stairs wind their way up, hedged in by iron railings, to dirty stained landings. Around the back a high wall cuts off the light and frames a long dark corridor, where children trail about, kicking at the rubbish when they haven't a ball.

This is women's territory. The few men around work on their cars or flit in and out of the house between work.

There are certain well-defined routes to this place. Joy Foster, a lone black mother, arrived here when the housing department pressurised her into accepting one of the flats by saying she might have to wait six months for another offer. Others arrive here from mental hospitals or in flight from brutal husbands. Whatever the route, the end result is the same. Those who deviate most from the administrators' idea of the respectable white working class and those who have been most severely battered by the repeated blows of capitalist urban life are concentrated here. This is the 'life sentence'—for once you are in here, it is very hard to get out.

But for some women even a life in Wynn House, on a poverty wage from the DHSS, comes as a respite from the intimidation and violence they experienced at men's hands before arriving here. It is only now becoming public knowledge, through the struggle of battered women, how widespread and brutal is the violence done to women and children inside the haven of family life. However, the escape route of leaving a man to live alone in the inner city does not create a permanent sanctuary from male violence.

132

In many ways fear seems an integral part of Wynn House—the fear of the violence of the other children on the block, of being abandoned by one's children when they grow up, of the sub-culture of male violence which is at its highest in the inner city.[15] No, here in Wynn House, having your own front door is not an absolute protection from the violence the city itself incorporates and displays in its central pornographic districts.

Jean Davis, who lives with her five children in one of the basement flats, describes to us the conception of her twins:

> I hated people then. I never hated till I became pregnant
> then—because of how I had conceived. Because I was pregnant
> with this person who I had no intention of going with—I didn't see
> him as no potential boyfriend or anything and I didn't like him
> sexually. There was no feeling as far as I was concerned . . . I locked
> myself up in the bathroom of my flat, thinking he had gone. Twice.
> And the third time he pounced on me. I dug so much skin off him,
> I have never fought with my fingers like that or bitten. The first
> time I had really felt hatred towards anyone. The first time I had
> felt I could kill anyone . . . I still see him. He just comes to pester.
> He says he comes to see the boys, but really he comes to pester me.
> Whenever I see him it puts up my blood pressure I hate him so.
> And its not making it any easier to look after the twins . . . I just
> can't be bothered with them, and half the reason is when he comes
> he just triggers off something inside my brain.

Jean Davis did not go to the police about this rape. As a lone black mother who had let a man into her flat she has little confidence that they would treat it as a crime. All the strands which twist together to make up the net of sexual and racial oppression bind together here into a noose[15] and the assaulted ones fear both the attacks and their consequences.

It is an afternoon in May. The flat is quite dark. Jean is sitting talking with her new baby in her arms. Every few minutes John and the twins burst in to ask questions, bringing her things they have discovered in her suitcase, emphasising the meaning of her words:

> I'm not me as a person any more. I'm just what they want me to be,
> I can't get a chance to be myself any more. They won't let me. Do
> you know—I have it right through the 24 hours. They wake me up
> in the night and if I'm not there, it's out of bed. If I'm in the toilet
> and Donald wakes up he comes shouting for me, he won't rest until
> he sees me. Daniel he gets up and crawls into bed until he finds me.

It is a particular form of isolation which faces lone parents at home with young children. Each way they turn there are the demands of children who always, closeted with the same parent in the same rooms make ever more strident demands for attention. And the parent knows that if only they felt less desperate, less hemmed in by the children, if they had a chance to be themselves once in a while, they could give the child those few moments of undivided attention which would bring some peace. But there's no one to turn to, to lean on, to be looked after by. Looking after begins and ends with the lone parent. And so the vicious circle continues. Parent and child wind each other up, stoking each other into a climax of clawing need.

The faces of the women of Wynn House betray the endless circles of denial isolation imposes—resigned yet tortured, impassive over the anger, submerged but still struggling. And with time the twin poles of anger and despair deepen; the world outside becomes ever more distant and unreal. And therefore even more frightening. As isolation spurs on isolation, confidence ebbs and the anger turns inwards in bitterness and self-doubt. This too is the prison sentence.

Maria Evans, a single black mother with one child, is surviving on an allowance from social security.

> Here I am, bored out of my bloody, tiny mind. And when you get to bed you're thinking about all sorts of bloody things. Like you're thinking: I wonder if my kid thinks I'm doing my best and I know I am. But to the other people it looks like you don't do nothing. It looks as if you're quite contented to sit here and live off the bloody government.

In Wynn House it is a constant battle to ward off the definitions of failure which have been framed in relation to motherhood. And the definitions all interlock; a woman without a man, a child without a father; either you're not looking after your kids properly because you've no job and no money, or you're selfishly going out to work and abandoning the children. Each way you turn there's a judgement of failure to greet you, and yet to bear the weight of raising children year in year out without the help of another is both a very demanding job and a very heavy responsibility.

Single parents, instead of receiving emotional and moral support for this labour of love, are on the end of a cultural assault which requires them daily to fight to assert their worth against the values of a male dominated society. Moira Mcguinn, a woman squatting in Wynn House with her two teenage children, felt this strongly:

> If you're a one parent family especially, and there's no man in the house, and you're a woman on your own with the children . . .

authorities have tried to step into the breach by funding after-care facilities. But these hostels now exist in a permanent state of siege—because they only have enough beds to meet a tiny fraction of the demand and because doctors and administrators use them as a dumping ground as they strive to achieve their discharge targets. What is specific to single homeless people is that their abandonment is publicly visible and that they are rejected according to the widely held notion that they have fallen through the floor of our society by virtue of their own failures and inablities. The welfare state's institutions resolve conflicts in such a way as to reinforce the passivity of its clients; it is incapable of solving social problems through stimulating self-activity—so in its dealings with the single homeless it eschews the only action which would allow them to begin to solve their own problems through their own self-activity—providing decent housing.

In the last thirty years the changing balance of state provision and abandonment has shifted according to changing economic circumstances and the balance of class forces. At different times the welfare state reveals different faces to different sections of the population. For the old in the sixties the benign face of Dr. Jekyll was prominent. Then it seemed more and more probable that pensioners' dreams of ending their days in comfort and dignity might be realised with state help. In the seventies Mr Hyde is to be seen more and more frequently. He was at work in the Town Hall, deciding on the cuts to be made, when old Mr Flood died alone in a GLC block of flats. Three months later his decomposed body was discovered after the neighbours had complained of the smell and the flies.[24]

As the numbers of old people have grown—by a million in the last ten years—so have governments sought to cut back social spending by getting the 'community' to look after the old, the sick and the disturbed. But the government invocations of good neighbourliness won't halt the 'community's' journey to extinction. A recent government survey of the elderly highlights how far down the road we've gone: a quarter of those interviewed in this nationwide survey named the insurance man as their only visitor in the previous six months; two-thirds of the ill or homebound interviewed never talk to the people next door.[25]

The provision of social services to the elderly is hinged around the aim of providing a minimum of care to keep old people out of institutions through the twin means of interventionist medicine and home helps, district nurses and meals on wheels. The attraction of these solutions lies in their low cost—a quarter to a third of the cost of institutionalising old people in council homes. But their cheapness does not mean they are comprehensive: in the mid seventies before the major cuts in public spending nearly four-fifths of those aged 75 or over never received a visit from a home nurse. Those who support the government's policies like to suggest that the choice is between dehumanising institutional care or caring support from the community growing out of real personal relationships. But the real choice facing many old people, and particularly those in the Inner city, is one between institutional care or a life of 'independence' weighed down with loneliness, poverty and isolation. Mr Flood's death was the culmination of a very isolated old age.

In contrast to the elderly and single homeless, the state's relationship to the family with growing children shows its intervention into working class social life in one of its most developed forms. The architects of the welfare state understood the central importance of the family as the cradle of social relations. The Beveridge report was unambiguous:

> In any measure of social policy in which regard is had to the facts the great majority of married women must be regarded as occupied on work which is vital though unpaid without which their husbands could not do their paid work and without which the whole nation could not continue.

Thereafter while the working class wanted an all round raising of living standards in order to be able to get the most out of married life, the eyes of the state were focusing ever more intently on what was going on inside the family. Truancy, juvenile crime and problem families came up for concerned comment in report after report in the fifties and sixties. The Plowden Report (1960), for example, said: 'It has been recognised that education is concerned with the whole man: henceforth it must be concerned with the whole family'. The state had been buttressing the family with allowances, supplements and free school milk, but now it seemed that a more regulative function was needed. Margaret Wynn, an influential voice of this new orthodoxy, put it this way:

> In the course of a lifetime a well trained man may add £100,000 or sometimes much more to a country's flow of goods and services. Whether or not he does so does not depend only on his education but also upon his upbringing from his early childhood. Some men add little to the wealth of the community, some cost the state thousands of pounds . . . The satisfactory rearing of children may continue to provide its reward for fifty or sixty years.[26]

From all quarters attention was now directed at mothers and their children, by psychologists like Bowlby, the child guidance clinics and educationalists and by the armies of social workers who were being trained in family case work. The social services have come to devote a large proportion of their budgets and their most skilled workers to regulating the reproduction of the next generation of wage labourers.

In its open regulation of family life the welfare state shows itself to be centrally concerned with the reproduction of capitalist social relations. And this concern is evident not only in its most authoritarian and repressive bodies, but in every sphere of its activity. Even in the state's most obviously 'progressive' acts, as when it moves to prevent child battering, it does so in an essentially authoritarian and bureaucratic fashion—denying the rights and needs of the children involved as it resolves the problem institutionally—through children's homes or often randomly assigned foster parents. The network of children's homes has expanded as family and community life has decayed, but the state as parent has proved all too often incapable of meeting the children's emotional needs. It regularly fails to assuage the sense of failure experienced by children who live outside the family; and that is hardly surprising since that is society's judgement of children's homes. Listen to the voice of a child in care:

> When I think about being adopted—and I wanted to be adopted when I was younger but the Council wouldn't agree to it—when I think of adoption I think it's one of the big hurdle things ahead of you. If it fails—if you're not adopted—what's the point of living?You're in a house where you're downgraded and if you can't be adopted by substitute parents, you've actually failed in life because you're given that chance. And that's the only thing that makes you closer to human than anything else—belonging to a family—and if you keep failing, that's when you start to depress yourself.[27]

The number of children in care has been steadily rising through the sixties and seventies—from 61,600 children in England and Wales in 1959 to 99,600 in 1975. And this increase has been largely a city phenomenon—the percentage of children in the care of county councils was the same, 4.8 per 1,000 of the population under 18 in 1962 as it was in 1973. And once again it is the inner city boroughs which have the highest proportion of children in care. In London, whilst a few middle class suburban boroughs like Richmond actually took proportionally less children into care in 1976 than they did in 1966 (down from 5.2/1,000 to 4.6/1,000), over the same decade, Hackney increased its proportion from 11.4 to 19.2, Lambeth from 12.1 to 20.8 and Camden from 13.3 to 19.2. But the top prizes for vigilance have to go to Kensington and Chelsea with 25.7/1,000 and Tower Hamlets with a staggering 31.5/1,000 in 1976.[28]

These spatial differences arise from two interlocking factors. First, the greater decay of community and family structure in the inner city means that many parents have no one but the state to turn to in critical situations. Thus the most frequent reason for children to be taken into care is the illness or confinement for childbirth of a parent. In the year to April 1975, these reasons caused 2,465 children, out of a total of 6,371, to be taken into care in the Inner London boroughs. Second, it is in the inner city that the crisis has produced the greatest concentration of rebellious youth, the largest numbers of juvenile arrests, a veritable flood of truanting school students—demanding a response from all the institutions of the state from social services to police departments and magistrates courts. But children can be taken into care for far less obvious reasons than these instances of delinquency. There is also growing evidence that social workers are imposing their white middle class values of what a desirable family life should be on urban families who do not fit their stereotypes[29] In particular, social service departments are keen to investigate one parent families, especially if they are black and the family deviates in any other way from the happy family ideal. There have been a number of cases in London where single parents have approached social service departments for practical help with their children only to find the situation turned on its head—the help they ask denied, and the extreme course of breaking up the family by taking the kids into care to solve 'the problem' pursued.

The social relations established between social services staff and their clients are so permeated with the values of this society that the very act of asking for help defines the client as inadequate and in need of investigation and regulation. In thirty cases investigated by an independent assessment service set up by MIND, the panel agreed with the local authority decision to take the children into care in only three. In particular they considered that councils did not take the cultural background of the families into account. 'If you're trying to define what's in the best interests of children, how do you do it?' asked Ron Lacy of MIND 'What factors do you bring to bear: the expectations of a white middle class family or something else?'

The welfare state reveals the contradictions at its heart when it's at its most caring. The beginnings of a struggle by children in council care is challenging the very nature of this state service and is making public the ways kids in care live and see themselves. Shifted from one social worker to another, shuttled in and out of children's homes, dumped on foster parents, deprived of the skills of survival, they are booted out on their eighteenth birthday. 'They plan your life for you and they don't let you come to your reviews and then all of a sudden they say, "Goodbye" '.

The state, in its welfare aspects, presents us with a familiar dilemma: we need its services for there are no other forces which can intervene to protect children, provide meals on wheels, or supply special schools for disabled children. But its cross-class origins, the bureaucratic framework in which these services operate, their overall strategic orientation, make them at best a distorted shadow of their potential for human liberation—and at worst a cudgel to enforce the sort of social relations government decides are in the best interests of capitalism as a whole. The evolution of the welfare state in the post-war period, the proliferation of its institutions under the control of the professional middle class, tended to reinforce the illusion that the state is a neutral body doing its best to balance conflicting, legitimate interests in a difficult situation.

However the class nature of the welfare state is shown not only by the way widely varying resources are allocated to different groups in the population, but also by the contradictions which prevent it creating a human environment for those it institutionalises. It is also revealed by the way in which its organs isolate, redefine and treat problems and crises issuing directly out of material conditions. The problem redefined, the causes individualised, the solution takes the form, to an increasing extent, of a medical fix. The form of help most easily available to the women of Wynn House is not childcare, nor an increased income, nor decent housing. It is help in the form of mood-changing pills, which do not resolve, but contain, individualise and even suppress realisation that a problem exists.

The pace of medicalising reactions to oppression has perceptibly quickened over the recent past. To long-established disease categories such as depression and anxiety new ones such as sociopathic behaviour and hyperactivity have been added. The sufferers of this last crippling disease are children, the symptoms, rebelliousness, unruly and undisciplined behaviour at home and school, and truancy. In Britain 1979 was the year when the Royal College of Psychiatrists launched a campaign to publicise the large numbers of people who were alchohol dependent—estimated at 0.5 of a million—which was also aimed at persuading the public that alchoholism was not a response to the realities of their lives, but a disease which should be medically treated. Such a medicalisation of this facet of the social crisis individualises a situation which is rapidly becoming a standing indictment of capitalist urbanism. One fact gives us an indication of the problem: in Westminster 31.8 per cent of the men and 28.3 per cent of the women presenting routinely to a GP's surgery in the area had enzyme levels which would suggest that they had habitually consumed half a bottle of whisky or its equivalent or more daily during the previous six weeks.[30]

Even more insidious is the overt use of the health service to control the family size of the surplus population. In some run down areas of Glasgow and the East End of London, third world women and white working class women who have been classified as 'unreliable' contraceptive users are being injected with Depo Provera, a long acting contraceptive.[31] This drug is known to have extremely dangerous and unpleasant side-effects both in the short and long-term, and has not been approved for general use in the US or in Britain by the Committee of Safety of Drugs. The doctors who prescribe Depo Provera are only putting into practice Sir Keith Joseph's judgement that the surplus population is made up of 'people we cannot afford'.

The cyclone of social change that has enveloped family life in the post-war period has both destroyed working class extended families and progressively fractured ever larger numbers of the nuclear units that succeeded them. As this has happened the working class has effectively lost the haven of family life which acted as a shield against the harshness of capitalist urban life. It has also lost the extended family culture which—although riven by the contradiction of patriarchy—possessed a solidarity in class terms in that, as occasion demanded, it would close ranks to repel the agents of ruling class authority. The negative effects of both this loss and modern family break-up bear down on the many people in the inner city, where daily life is at its most radically removed from the cosy world of the pretty poster family. As economic stagnation engenders cutbacks in public spending and as new ways of disciplining the surplus population are sought out by the state, the welfare lifelines are hauled in and 'personal problems' are screwed to a new pitch.

There is another side to these developments. As the nuclear

family breaks up, and more and more people live outside its structures, so the possibilities for establishing new systems of informal solidarity grow. The journey to a dump estate whether it originated on a West Indian island or a semi-detached in Hounslow will always involve very real material oppressions, but it may well also create the possibility of reforming cultures of resistance and solidarity. At present we can see these most fully developed in the black community, which has both inherited a long history of resistance strategies under colonialism[32] and whose social life has had to resist the ravages of a racist society.

We need a break with an economistic approach to the welfare state which emphasises the need to simply increase the quantity of the services to the working class. We have to challenge the very nature of these services and the ways bureaucratic agencies define, and impose their definition, of the social services' needs of any particular district. We have to raise the question of the local working class defining its own needs—and in that process—redefining the nature of the services which are required.

Within the labour movement itself, it is beginning to be accepted that the mass support for Tory policies at the election and the apathetic response to subsequent economic cuts, indicates the deep disillusionment amongst the working class towards the welfare state. An approach which seeks to maintain the status quo by defending the existing level of services cannot reverse such apathy and hostility. Nor can the problem be overcome by arguing for increased public spending on social services, if the welfare state's features of bureaucracy, control, and regulation of the social life of the working class are not challenged. We will be returning to these questions in our conclusion but before doing so must consider the relationship between certain groups in the surplus population and the repressive apparatus of the state.

6. From Consent to Coercion: The State and the Surplus Population

> when yu fling mi inna prison
> I did warn yu
> when you kill Oluwale
> I did warn yu
> when yu beat Joshua Francis
> I did warn yu
>
> when yu pick pan de Panthers
> I did warn yu
> when yu jack mi up gainst de wall ha didn't bawl
> but I did warn yu.
>
> now yu si fire burning in mi eye,
> smell badness pan mi breat,
> feel vialence, vialence,
> burstin outta mi;
> look out!
>
> it too late now:
> I did warn yu.

From *Time Come* by Linton Kwesi Johnson[1]

The power of the capitalist state is rooted in its ability to quash opposition by force, but it does not fulfill its role as the guardian of class divisions necessary for capitalist activity by a simple and continuous resort to violence and repression. This was stressed by the Italian Marxist Antonio Gramsci, who analysed the way in which the state maintains and reproduces capitalist social relations both through its use of force and, equally importantly, by promoting popular consent for its own rule and hence the established order. This popular consent is created in multifarious ways as the state provides an organising direction, a coherence, for the whole of civil society—through formal representation in the parliamentary system, through its educational and cultural organisations, through its use of the mass media and through its 'welfare state' activities. In each historical period there is a particular combination of the two poles of state activity. But in general, during times of relative social peace, the coercive and consent-creating wings of state activity are interdependent and reinforcing—coercive interventions, which tend to be limited, are highly successful precisely because they are underwritten by the majority's broad consent.

But, Gramsci argued, periods of economic and social crisis precipitate a tilt in the operation of the state away from consent towards the pole of coercion. When such a shift occurs:

> The forms of state intervention become more overt and direct. Consequently such moments are also marked by a period of 'unmasking' The masks of liberal consent and popular consensus slip to reveal the reserves of coercion and force on which the cohesion of the state and its legal authority finally depends . . . This tends to further polarise the 'crisis of hegemony' since the state is progressively drawn down, now in its own name, into the arena of struggle and direction.[2]

But in such a period the more naked use of state power threatens to spread the very loss of consent which is part and parcel of the complex of social and economic crisis that has occasioned the tilt towards the pole of coercion. The forces of repression are then in a dangerously isolated situation, their operations no longer underwritten by popular consent. Thus reorganising consent around a more repressive state apparatus through the promotion of a new more authoritarian consensus becomes a crucial task.

In Britain the seventies ended with an electoral victory for a party of the radical right superficially committed to 'rolling back' state intervention. This commitment, however, refers solely to a programme of truncating state regulation of the economy and decreasing state provision of goods and services for poorer sections of the working class. Its necessary counterpart is an equally deep commitment to strengthening the repressive apparatus of the state so that the consequences of its economic strategy in terms of social crisis and political opposition can be contained. As Stuart Hall remarked in a 1979 lecture:

> Make no mistake about it: under this regime the market is to be free, the people are to be disciplined . . . Its preferred slogan is 'Free Economy: Strong State' . . . It is the Liberty of property and of contract, of unbridled market forces, and of competitive man and 'possessive individualism' to which this slogan refers. It is not the 'Liberty' of those who have nothing to sell but their labour.[3]

Since May 1979 the intense anti-union propaganda of the late seventies has been transformed into new legislation attacking the ability of workers to take action in support of others and restricting the freedom to picket. New racist and sexist immigration controls have been introduced, rights of appeal against deportation are being cut down and the existing police/immigration service powers to conduct witchhunts for 'illegals' have been put to wider use. As mass unemployment becomes a reality, the pursuit of 'welfare scroungers' increases. As public expenditure is cut, the proportion of it devoted to the armed forces and the police is rising—so enabling them to recruit the labour and buy the equipment necessary for policing high unemployment.

Every week state functionaries are to be heard attacking 'subversive elements' who dare to criticise police methods; and every week ruling class efforts to summon up a new authoritarian consensus become more transparent. This list could be extended, and when all the elements are considered together it is tempting to conclude that the tilt towards coercion has been a rapid development primarily associated with the Tory government. This would be a mistake, however, for the tilt towards the pole of coercion in the operations of the British state progressed throughout the seventies in response to a loss of consent among various groups in the population. Within the context of a sharply deteriorating world market situation this shift occurred, we would argue, under the impact of four major influences: the intensifying struggle of the oppressed Catholic minority in Northern Ireland, which led to armed insurrection in the early seventies; the resurgence of militancy on the part of a wide section of the industrial working class that scuppered the Heath administration's attempts to directly regulate wage bargaining by use of the courts; the failure of existing mechanisms for disciplining a generation of working class youth, whose material position and prospects have changed rapidly for the worse; and the intransigent refusal of black people to suffer passively the consequences of the economic and social crisis.

The starting point of our argument in this chapter is firstly an observation that the activity of each of these groups has had a distinct bearing on the restructuring of the state apparatus of control and repression; and, secondly, a judgement that the split between the surplus population (embracing many Catholics in Northern Ireland, many working class youth and many of Britain's black population) and the rest of the working class has been and is a major facilitating factor in the creation of a new authoritarian consensus. Before examining this in much greater detail it is worthwhile reminding ourselves how far down the road we have already travelled.

Today special no-jury courts for 'terrorist' offences are an integral part of the legal system in Northern Ireland. They were introduced as a sop to international criticism of the previous system of internment by executive order. It is now clear from evidence given by a prominent member of the Police Surgeons' Association that 80 per cent of the convictions handed down in these closed rooms are based on confessions extracted by brutalising suspects.[4] In Republican strongholds, such as South Armagh, only elite units of the occupying army can maintain regular operations—despite the state's much vaunted attempts at 'Ulsterisation'. Demonstrations in the cities—rather than being politely shepherded through the streets by unarmed police—frequently have to be banned, met with army barricades, water cannon, rubber bullets, gas and even on occasion live ammunition. With incredibly detailed information on 40 per cent of the population now recorded on an army computer (itself linked into the social security information network and those of other government departments) surveillance and intelligence gathering is virtually the only growth industry in the province.[5]

On the mainland, the four years of the Heath administration provided ample demonstration of the simple truth that determined opposition by a sufficiently wide section of the organised working class can render parliament's laws inoperable. The development of mass and flying pickets during the struggle against the Industrial Relations Act both wrecked the government's strategy and, by defeating the policing exercises, exposed the inability of the law and order apparatus to repress militant trade union activity. The laws themselves had to be repealed—not least because their very existence threatened to undermine working class consent to the rule of law as a whole. For five years after 1974, the Labour government did much to hold the conflict between capital and labour in check, but the memory of the tumultuous events of the early seventies, exposing problems of control over mass action so sharply, continued to exert a powerful influence over the restructuring of the state apparatus. As a result, as new restrictive legislation reaches the statute book, the police are emerging from six years of intense training designed to equip them for controlling public order situations arising out of workplace conflicts.

During Labour's period of office the state was faced with growing problems of social control in the inner cities, where the impact of recession has been such as to create widespread unemployment among white as well as black youth, where rocketing juvenile crime and vandalism is concentrated, where problems of discipline in the schools are at their most intense, and where the growth of a white working class oppositional youth culture (punks, skins) is most evident. Such trends have provided subject matter for the shrill cries of the law and order brigade seeking to mobilise public opinion behind a more authoritarian consensus. Unchecked by the efforts of the state's soft cop social and educational workers, these developments have led to the burden of maintaining social control over youth in the inner areas falling to an even greater extent on the shoulders of the men in blue. And as their use of powers in this role has become more overt, the loss of consent among other groups in these areas has widened. Thus an ORC poll on attitudes to the police conducted in April 1980 showed that while a majority of the North-West's population generally had confidence in the police, hostility to and distrust of the police was high in Huyton (Merseyside) and Mosside (Manchester) and cut across both age and race divides.[6] It was no doubt observation of this trend, among others, that had led the Chief Constable of Merseyside to publicly state his belief the previous year that, if unemployment continued to rise at expected levels, martial law would soon be required to control the conurbation.

It is among Britain's Afro-Caribbean and Asian communities, however, that general consent in the face of the state's law and order apparatus has declined to the greatest degree on the mainland. This has been an uneven process—by generation, city and distinct national community—but it is one that has both accelerated and become generalised as the last ten years have passed. And as this has happened other state agencies charged with maintaining and reproducing capitalist social relations among the black population have progressively lost much of their tenuous influence. One indicator of this is the fact that almost every major incident of 'public disorder' on the streets of mainland Britain has involved members of the Afro-Caribbean and Asian communities as front-line combatants. Liverpool, Bradford, Birmingham, Leeds, Lewisham, Southall and Bristol—all have seen massed challenges to authority, usually spontaneous but often in a highly politicised form.

In April 1980, for example, when the Bristol police mounted a raid on the Black & White cafe, they were moving in on a meeting place of black unemployed youth on a weekday afternoon. It was one of the few such venues in the city not to have been closed down in the previous two years. Inside the cafe, among the thirty odd people there, was a group who were discussing travelling to London the next day to picket outside a court where a black student—originally from St. Pauls—was due to appear on a 'sus' charge. As news of the raid spread, a crowd quickly gathered outside that had no intention of allowing either the cafe owner, his customers or the cafe's contents to be taken away without a struggle. After hours of running battles the police were forced to withdraw, having suffered significant losses of equipment and a number of injuries. For four hours they were unable to assemble sufficient forces to re-enter the area and, even then, reportedly only did so after responding positively to a telephoned ultimatum demanding the immediate release of the cafe owner.[7]

The next day the press carried reports of 'black mobs on the rampage'—but during the hours when St. Pauls had been a 'no-go' area the looting had been highly selective and there was no inter-racial violence. The premises of well-liked local shopkeepers were spared; others, however, were either broken into and had the goods removed or they were fired. Both white youths and old age pensioners participated in the looting.[8] As a Baptist minister who saw the initial confrontations commented: 'Colour had nothing to do with this, I think it was a question of authority and reaction to authority, rather than a question of colour'.[9]

How has such a pitch of confrontation between the authority of the state and large sections of Britain's black communities been reached? In a nutshell the answer lies in the fact that black people in Britain have experienced the shift to coercion in the state's activities ahead of other sections of the mainland population, and have resisted it. This has happened, on the one hand, as the state has imposed successively harsher immigration controls in a period when British capital was re-orientating itself towards Europe. On the other hand it has occurred in response to a growing revolt of black youth against the subservient position in society demanded of them.

The state and immigration

In the years following the war, the future of Britain's colonies was a major problem for successive British governments. The threat of insurrection against colonial rule coincided with a highly unstable political situation in Europe and the East. In response the British state slowly embarked on preparing the ground for a formal granting of political independence to the majority of the remaining colonies within a framework, designed to ensure the continued domination of British capital in the economic life of these nations. This involved a delicate mixture of armed repression against the communist wings of the independence movements and negotiations with and support for, moderate nationalist leaders deemed capable of holding the line against widescale change.

It is in this context of prolonged national struggle in the colonies, that we should place the 1948 Nationality Act, which gave all citizens of the Empire and Commonwealth equal rights of entry and settlement in the UK. As such it continued the tradition of a unified Empire and strengthened the hand of moderate leaders in the colonies, at a time when it was becoming clear that migration of refugees from Europe would not satisfy the hunger for unskilled labour exhibited by a reviving peacetime economy. Other sources had to be found and this fitted in with the requirements of decolonisation.

The benefits of such an arrangement were clear—the shortage of labour would be met by an inflow of immigrants who would be consigned to the least popular and lowest paid jobs through the operations of the racist labour market; and the costs of raising the incoming labourers from cradle to labour exchange had already been met by the underdeveloped economy.

Up to the end of the 1950s, when the European economies were beginning to organise immigrant labour on a carefully controlled contract basis, Britain remained committed to free entry for all Commonwealth citizens. By then, however, the most powerful sectors of British capital were moving in line with a general trend amongs all industrialised countries to invest in developed rather than in underdeveloped territories. The boardrooms of some of the most powerful UK companies were starting to concentrate their energies on the Common Market, and it was becoming clear that entry to the EEC and an operative 1948 Nationality Act were incompatible. The question of immigration controls thus became more urgent as pressure to join Europe grew and this was reinforced by racist electoral pressure. With much of the Empire firmly on the road to neo-colonialism, the Tories announced their intention to introduce restrictions.

The 1962 Act introduced a system under which potential immigrants had to obtain a work voucher before they or their dependants could freely enter and settle. Over the next nine years governments of both parties brought Britain into line with the EEC as, step by step, restrictions on the issue of vouchers were tightened and racial distinctions were introduced into the control of commonwealth immigration. Each step was both facilitated by and itself encouraged a mounting wave of public racism, until—with a new Act in 1971—the European model of immigration controlled on a contract basis was achieved. When it came into force in 1973, it eliminated the rights of black Commonwealth citizens to settle in the UK. From then on entry via work permit gave no right of settlement. Britain had completed its separation from the Commonwealth in the sense that the black migrant had become a guestworker, only able to enter 'on a permit to a specific job in a specific place for a period of not longer than twelve months. He could not change his job without the permission of the government— which meant that he was dependent on his employer for the recommendation: he had to be a good little wage slave.'[10]

When the 1971 Act came into force all 'primary' immigration into Britain ceased, and subsequently the only black immigrants who were allowed to settle were close relations of those already there and such special groups as male fiances and East African UK passport holders. It is the rights of these people and of black settlers who still have family members overseas that were steadily eroded in the rest of the seventies, and were dealt a further blow by the adoption of new racist and sexist legislation by the Thatcher government in 1980.

The erection of controls around harbours and airports gave the police a new role—that of detecting and expelling the illegal immigrant. As controls have become tighter and the ideological attack on black people has developed, so police powers of internal control over black people have grown. Under the 1971 Act they have the power to detain and deport without trial or any effective right of appeal. The numbers so treated have steadily increased in line with a strengthening of the illegal immigrant squads. In recent years there have been a substantial number of cases of bona fide UK citizens being incarcerated for months in prisons or detention centres without there being any form of judicial hearing or any evidence of their illegal entry. The numbers actually detained, however, represent the tip of the iceberg as regards the number of black people who are questioned, harassed through passport checks and indirectly disciplined by the police use of their unfettered powers under the Immigration Acts. For some time it has been the view of the Institute of Race Relations that 'the police as a growing general practice, are acting on the assumption that black people are illegal immigrants until they can prove otherwise'[11] In the East End of London, for example, those Asians who have reported racist attacks to the police have frequently found they were far more interested in their passport and immigration status than the committed crime. They have also systematically harassed Asians trying, in the absence of effective police protection, to protect themselves. 1980 (in the aftermath of Southall, Bristol and the new immigration laws) has seen an upsurge of large-scale raids on Asian businesses and places of work carried out in military style by the police and immigration service. During these 'fishing expeditions' large numbers of people who had committed no offence were detained and treated in a deliberately intimidatory fashion.

In the post-war period the free movement of citizens in and out of the nations of the Commonwealth was a laissez-faire luxury for the British state tolerated for relatively short-term strategic reasons. Once the state, at capital's behest, became centrally involved in EEC entry, it was inevitable that successive governments would have to engage in sealing off all the entrances to the British market which had previously been open to blacks. Each successive stage of this development had the effect of quickening the deep currents of racism originating in the imperial past and still infusing all aspects of social life in Britain. It has also brought the state into a distinct and confrontational relationship with the black settler population and their children—both because it has involved an attack on the democratic rights of particular individuals, and because it has been a major influence in shifting the state apparatus into a coercive relationship with the black population as a whole.

Black youth against society—the police against black people

In the fifties Britain held out the promise of a welcome alongside a job, and maybe education and training, to immigrants from both the Indian subcontinent and the Caribbean. The advertisements in the post offices of the West Indies were unambiguous: HELP BUILD YOUR MOTHER COUNTRY. There was little or no work on the islands. The USA had slammed the door. There were few alternatives and a long tradition of migrating for work. But the end of the journey proved Britain to be no mother country. As Gus John has written:

> We came with false hopes and misguided notions nurtured by the colonialists' teaching of the great land Britain was and its

preparedness to extend its open arms to its needy and deserving subjects whose own lands it had systematically left underdeveloped. What we were not taught was that racism was endemic to Britain and had been its greatest economic weapon for hundreds of years.[12]

Consigned to the lowest rungs of the labour ladder, effectively excluded from the trade union movement, finding accomodation in rundown boarding houses or the worst available rented housing, the West Indian and Asian communities had to organise themselves in the major English cities surrounded by a climate of hostility and indifference. It was a rude awakening, and the prelude to a long struggle begun by many in the belief that acceptance could gradually be achieved and intolerable racism effectively combated within the limits of the law.

Over the years houses were bought, places of worship established, clubs and small businesses begun, skilled jobs sought and factories organised. By the mid-sixties, however, with the state promoting racist immigration laws, 'increasing police harassment, particularly of West Indians, mounting discrimination in employment and housing and the relegation of West Indian children to ESN (educationally sub-normal) schools sparked off militant struggles in the Caribbean community. The black movement in America gave a fillip to black nationalism'.[13] At the same time factory organisation drives carried out by the Indian Workers Association gave notice that the Asian communities were also adopting a more actively political response to their problems.

The state responded to these developments with weak anti-discrimination legislation and the creation of bodies specifically aimed at bolstering consent among the black communities by absorbing discontent. As such, the strategy sought to reinforce the reluctance of many immigrants to abandon the belief that justice and advancement could be achieved by moderation, and create a situation whereby those who took militant action outside the state-organised framework could be effectively repressed without producing a significant backlash in the black community. This arrangement worked reasonably well until the early seventies. But since then—despite the production of slightly tougher anti-discrimination legislation and reconstituted co-optive bodies in 1976—it has progressively broken down. This has happened as economic stagnation has borne down disproportionately hard on a black working class increasingly inclined to militancy in the workplace; as black communities have moved towards organising their own defence in the face of racist violence; and as the refusal of sections of black youth to accept the framework of racist/capitalist social relations has brought them into sharp conflict with the police.

This refusal first emerged on a large scale among West Indian youth. It was a refusal on many levels—taking different forms for different individuals. A refusal to simply weather the odds doing the shit work which was expected on public transport, at Ford or in the hospitals. It was a refusal to suffer passively, to go quietly when the man said so, to allow the arrest of fellows to go unopposed. A refusal to cloak blackness with white culture. It was also a refusal to follow in their parents' footsteps:

> I am not going to work at a place for forty years and not have anything to show for it. After forty years they just have a little watch. And one man owns a house and he alone lives there, and the house is so big with all 200 rooms and I have to walk the streets. That's not right.[14]

This is a generation that by and large has no other homeland to dream of returning to, and a voice that is both conscious of being rejected by a racist and capitalist society and has rejected a 'normal life' of waged labour within it.

Such a stand was made possible through the development of an oppositional culture in the black neighbourhoods:

> The winning away of cultural space in which an alternative black society could flourish . . . here began the 'colonisation' of certain streets, neighbourhoods, cafes and pubs, the growth of the revivalist churches, midday hymn singing and mass baptisms in the local swimming baths, the spilling out of Caribbean fruit and vegetables from the Indian shops, the shebeen and the Saturday night blues party, the construction of the sound systems.[15]

The establishment of these black neighbourhoods opened up for some the possibility of surviving by alternative means, by a process of hustling involving activities such as gambling, undeclared part-time work, ganja selling, shoplifting, street crime, housebreaking and distributing stolen goods. Sections of the white working class have long chosen to survive through similar strategies, demonstrating in their communities a collective contempt for work discipline, concern for and dependence on the good-will of an employer and outside authority.[16] By the early seventies a significant section of West Indian youth represented a threat in the eyes of authority, not simply because they were part of a swelling number of wageless urban youth but primarily because they were developing a collective solidarity. In doing so, they could draw strength from a culture which counterposed the struggle for survival in the face of oppression to the state's label of 'lazy vicious little criminals'.[17]

Within the development of a broad Caribbean culture, West Indian youth rebel culture demonstrated its vitality with the phenomenal growth of the sound systems. They played a music expressive of direct opposition to integration into white society and subservience before it. The pursuit of activities so directly at odds with the desirable behaviour of a well disciplined workforce, and the growing sense of righteous solidarity among black youth, soon attracted attention from the police who took to trying to reassert their authority at the venues where wageless youth gathered. By early 1976 pitched battles between police and youths had occurred at a large number of these places—at South London reggae festivals, at five or six London clubs, and at the Leeds bonfire night. There were also countless raids on blues parties and persistent harassment of any rendezvous that served as a base for community action, like Notting Hill Gate's Mangrove restaurant.

The slightest resistance to a police presence was the occasion for calling in massive reinforcements, sealing off the area, wading in with boots and truncheons, and arresting a dozen or so as the premises were cleared. And resistance there was, as—in marked contrast to habitual white working class response to the police—arrests were physically opposed. By 1976 this had become such a common phenomenon that the Metropolitan Police, in evidence to the Select Committee on Race Relations and Immigration, singled it out for special mention:

> Recently there has been a growth in the tendency for members of London's West Indian communities to combine against the police officers who are effecting the arrest of a black person or who are in some way enforcing the law in situations which may involve black people. In the last twelve months forty such incidents have been recorded.[18]

Each policing exercise in a black area was becoming a test of strength between two polarising forces. The mass trials which resulted from these confrontations also became the occasion for establishing defence campaigns which reached deep into the black communities and successfully mobilised to win many acquittals.

These middle years of the seventies were a time when international recession loomed on the horizon, when working class living standards began to decline, and when scapegoating voices were thundering about immigrants and muggers. Fascist groups began to grow in numbers and influence, and racist violence against black people, homes, businesses and meeting places increased. All the strands around the policing of black youth, the growth of racial violence and the 'undesirability' of immigrants, tightened into a knot during the spring and summer of 1976. It was a time of an extraordinary convergence of events.

In May the press manufactured a furore over the temporary housing of Asians expelled from Malawi in a luxury hotel. 'Migrants just here for welfare handouts' was a typical headline, and two days after the *Sun* led with 'Scandal of £600 a week immigrants' an Indian family's home was set on fire. Three days later the Greenwich Islamic Centre was broken into and ransacked. On the streets of the East End, as recorded by *Race Today* there were 23 serious assaults between 5 March and 21 May. In the May local elections half of the National Front's candidates received 10 per cent of the votes cast where they stood. On 22 May two black students were stabbed to death in East London. The murder of Gurdip Singh Chaggar in Southall on 4 June sparked off a powerful reaction amongst the Asian communities in both West and East London, and the Southall police station was besieged by Asian youth. The uprising of the youth of Soweto later in the summer had a further strong impact within the black communities just as the year culminated in the 1976 Carnival battle—'the worst outbreak of public disorder since the war'.

The battle which erupted on the last day of the Carnival was a serious reversal for the police. Virtually the entire Carnival turned out to support those that had taken on the police—there were very few amongst the quarter of a million attending who did not think the police were reaping the whirlwind of their own provocations during the first two days. The press coverage was almost universally critical of the police. The *Evening Standard* editorial declared:

> A force seven times as large as the one that attended last year's festivities must surely have contributed to the tension in a part of London in which, as the Yard well knows, the police are regarded as the natural enemy. The whole exercise was an error of judgement.[19]

It looked like one weekend's policing was going to blow away the carefully nurtured distinction between 'troublemaking youth' and the respectable majority of the West Indian community. The naked display of police power had done more to create solidarity between youth and the wider community than innumerable public meetings. This was the police 'error of judgement'—it had lost the consent of a sizeable section of the urban working class as it engaged in a test of strength with the West Indian community and lost.

The 1976 Carnival initiated a new phase in black/police relations. After this, recognition that press hysteria and open repression of the youth culture had only succeeded in deepening the loss of consent led to a change of tactics. This was reflected in a number of superficial developments such as an increase in the police community relations effort, a highly expensive and totally ineffective series of campaigns to attract black recruits and well advertised 'sensitive policing' at subsequent Carnival-type events. More significantly it was reflected in a general move away from initiating set-piece confrontations at West Indian and Asian cultural venues, an avoidance of group trials which provide opportunities for the campaigns to be mounted and the maintenance of discipline through increased use of individual harassment and summary charges carrying no right of jury trial. *Race Today* between the Septembers of 1974 and 1976 chronicled 12 major public clashes between the police and black people—all of which had led to multiple trials. However, between the 1976 Carnival and the summer of 1979 there were only two such trials.

For a number of reasons the change in police methods has not stopped the steady haemorrhaging of consent to their operations among the Afro-Caribbean and Asian communities. The economic crisis has swollen the number of youth unemployed, thus both deepening the crisis of social control in the inner urban immigrant communities and making it harder to control by a softly, softly approach. The introduction of saturation policing exercises in which given areas are blanketed for a period by mobile tactical squads has been one result. In addition the growth of the National Front has brought the police into a new public role as the prominent protector of a racist and fascist group. And when the provocations of the Front have met with mass resistance the forces of 'law and order' have once again seized the chance for savagely disciplining the threatened communities.

By the end of the seventies, the day-to-day experience of many of the older generation had also convinced them that youth had some justice on their side. The police failure to protect blacks from attacks and the massive force used to protect the Front have a bearing on this. In fact so blatant has state racism become that even the Commission for Racial Equality, in a 1979 Report on the East End, concluded that the police 'appear to have condoned organised attempts to incite racial hatred' and noted that there is a 'great breach' in public confidence in the willingness to treat citizens equally before the law.[20] However this mild level of criticism of one state body by another was not enough to convince community leaders they could resolve their problems by the working parties proposed by the Commission. It was denounced as 'a betrayal and an insult to the work we have done. After ignoring Brick Lane for eight years, they have produced the greatest wash out and cop out imaginable.'[21]

By June 1980 a new and potentially very important point in the nationwide process of polarisation had been reached when delegates from sixty black groups voted to campaign for a withdrawal of co-operation with the police over identity parades, recruitment and community liaison schemes.

It is highly unlikely that the police are in any sense ignorant of the possible consequences of their actions. The Metropolitan Police, for example, have a highly sophisticated understanding of the importance of creating consent to their authority. To take actions which lose them this consent is only done because no other course is possible—because structural contradictions have ensured that disciplining with the consent of the disciplined has become a progressively harder target to achieve. At the same time, sections of the black community have revolted against acceptance of *de facto* second class citizenship, and economic stagnation has precluded the granting of material benefits to the black working class which would have been the only viable basis for bolstering the influence of institutions designed to reproduce consent. And as attempts to channel dissent into malleable forms have broken down, harsher measures to directly discipline the black communities, the promotion of ideological campaigns against black people and connivance at racist attacks have come to play an increasing part in the state response. This in turn has broadened and deepened the loss of consent and, over time, led to the authority of the state being recognised for what it is and challenged on a mass scale.

Restructuring the state apparatus

The shift to a more authoritarian state form progressed throughout the seventies—but not in an open, linear fashion. Insurrection in Northern Ireland, industrial militancy, the crisis of social control in the inner cities all influenced the process, as the state responded to specific threats by promoting new laws, reshaping the security forces and introducing new methods of surveillance. Taken as a whole, these developments represent a 'tilt towards coercion' with serious consequences for the working class seeking to defend its interests in a long wave of stagnation. For, although the sharpest edges of the state's operations have so far been felt by minority groups, there can be little doubt that many recent changes have been effected with an eye to possible future conflict with the big battalions of the industrial working class. This gearing up of the law and order apparatus has occurred in an almost sub-terranean way without evoking strong opposition outside the arenas where consent has already foundered. In our view the divi-sion between the surplus population—and the divisions between different groups in the surplus population—have played an extremely important part in this process. Thus methods and procedures first applied in Northern Ireland with the passive approval of the mainland working class are now in use on the mainland; laws ostensibly passed to deal with 'terrorists' and other 'troublemakers' have arrived on the statute book as effective limitations on industrial action and political dissent; experience gained in disciplining the black communities opposing the National Front now stands the police in good stead when it comes to dealing with massed trade unionists. In the last parts of this chapter we examine how the triangular relationship of the surplus population, the working class and the state itself has facilitated the shift towards a more authoritarian state form.

Policing the inner city

During the seventies, the challenge to property relations and the smooth reproduction of capitalist social relations increasingly came from working class youth in general. The decade began with a fairly narrow set of youth singled out for attention—skinheads, hippies, student militants and blacks. There followed constant rumblings about vandalism, hooliganism and truancy and from 1976 onwards both media and state were glancing anxiously at the militancy and self-organisation of Asian youth. By the end of the decade politicians, media and state functionaries were talking of youth as a whole as being 'a problem'. The number of crimes recorded as committed by young people rose throughout the period, leading *The Times* to talk of 'an intractable issue of rising juvenile criminality'. By 1977, 51 per cent of all arrests in London involved people under 21 and 44 per cent of those arrested for burglaries were under 17. Youths between 17 and 21 now account for 25 per cent of the prison population.[22]

This progression has not, of course, been unconnected to the structural unemployment which was hitting black youth at the beginning of the period and is now bearing down on all working class youth. Loss of income through unemployment debars youth from almost all recreational and cultural activities which have to be bought in the marketplace and inevitably leads to problems of social control. As vandalism has become a routine recreational activity for younger kids and teenagers alike, thefts have risen and truancy has reached a level where one London Borough estimates between 450 and 600 kids skip school every day.

The state has been faced with an enormous problem, and to meet it the judiciary, the police and professional opinion has moved in a decidedly authoritarian direction. Repeated calls from all these groups have been made for repeal of the liberal Children and Young Persons Act (1969) which emphasised care and treatment for the young offender rather than discipline and punishment. Anderton, Chief Constable of Greater Manchester, for instance, has deemed that hooligans should 'be placed in penal work camps where through hard labour and unrelenting discipline they should be made to sweat as they have never sweated before'. The Tories in office set up tough detention centres on an experimental basis. And as the police have adopted more repressive responses on the street, so consent among a whole generation has begun to founder. Thus the National Youth Bureau has commented that the existence of 'fear, hostility and mistrust' between young people and the police is now almost universal. In the bureau's judgement this is a cross-class phenomenon—other surveys, however, suggest that in inner urban (and not only high immigrant) areas hostility to the police is at its greatest both among young people and the older generations.[23] One or two police chiefs like Alderson (Devon and Cornwall) have emphasised the need to revive 'community spirit' in rundown neighbourhoods. But the places where these experiments have had some success have either been in quite untypical small cities, such as Exeter, or in parts of conurbations where traditional policing methods have gone hand in hand with massive public expenditure. In the Gibbshill district of Glasgow, for example, vandalism and crime rates declined as a result of the efforts of four police on constant foot patrol and three million pounds of additional expenditure on housing, sports and recreational facilities. A significant extension of this strategy is quite clearly not on the agenda for the eighties.

In the absence of initiatives capable of either eradicating the causes of crime or of bolstering co-operation, the police have had to respond forcefully. One element of this has been the institution of saturation policing—usually carried out by the tactical reserve or Special Patrol Group of the force concerned. In London the SPG has been rotated round the Inner London divisions on month long tours designed to give the urban (and particularly black) working class a salutary lesson. Such exercises provide a highly visible and intimidating police presence as carriers cruise the streets, road blocks are set up and large numbers are stopped and searched at random. As early as summer 1975, the SPG's tour of Lambeth and Lewisham produced 14,000 stops without arrest and only 400 arrests—during these exercises a mass of low level intelligence has been gathered on people deemed to be suspicious.

The task force occupying Lambeth in autumn 1978 acted according to the familiar pattern; setting up roadblocks, enforcing an unofficial curfew on some estates and participating in a massive dry run of a counter insurgency operation. This started with the total sealing off of the heart of the West Indian community on a spurious excuse, and continued for several hours as people were ordered off the streets and houses were entered and searched without warrant. It is an indication of how far this breach between consent and coercion has opened that the local police commander rejected criticism of his failure to warn the police-community liaison committee of the SPG's arrival with the words: 'no good general ever declares his forces in a prelude to any type of attack'.[24]

As they move into an area the SPG act on the assumption that those who conform to certain stereotypes are in need of a lesson. In this, however, they are not alone—for both police and courts have provided ample evidence in recent years for the view that certain types of person are deemed guilty until proven innocent. The most notorious example of this has been the widespread use of the charge of being a suspected person under the 1824 Vagrancy Act by the Liverpool, Manchester and London police. This law—under which committing two suspicions but not criminal acts leads to conviction—is so manifestly oppressive that the Parliamentary Select Committee on Home Affairs unanimously called for its abolition in its first report. Significantly, out of forty bodies submitting evidence, only the Home Office and the Police Federation sought to defend the law. Both of these bodies know that the effectiveness of 'sus' as a tool of control lies in its deterrent message—if you hang around on the street corner it could be the start of a long criminal record. Conviction is near automatic with recent surveys putting the rate at around 95 per cent. This is a staggeringly high total given the fact that 80 per cent of the defendants plead not guilty—eloquent testimony to the fact that magistrates courts, in their mundane processes, rubber-stamp the convictions the police seek.

Police forces differ in their choice of summary charges. In the West Midlands for example, charges of attempted theft and behaviour likely to cause a breach of the peace are preferred to 'sus'. Nevertheless, the increased use of summary charges appears to be a widespread phenomenon that has been encouraged by the 1976 Criminal Law Act, which enlarged the number of charges carrying no right to jury trial heard in the magistrates courts. In these arenas defendants have no right to know in advance the nature of the case they must answer and the granting of legal aid is entirely discretionary. The switch to summary charges has been partly determined by sheer pressure of numbers in an attempt to prevent the court system breaking down—but it also has a strategic dimension in avoiding jury trials around which defence campaigns can be mobilised. Thus the police charged over 90 per cent of the 350 people arrested at Southall with summary offences.[25] Group trials were refused despite the fact that many defendants had common witnesses and the possibility of solidarity was further weakened by sending the defendants to a distant court. In dispensing 'justice' the magistrates made it quite clear on several occasions that mere presence at the demonstration was a pointer to guilt.

There is also evidence that police use summary charges to prevent scrutiny of their own methods by juries. Thus a solicitor wrote to *The Guardian* that:

> It is a common experience that most solicitors can confirm that if a client is beaten up by the police, and suffers severe injuries, a charge of assault on the police results (in which an officer has invariably suffered a minor scratch or an alleged kick from which there is little or no bruising); and the police know that since the chances of conviction are in the 85-95 per cent probability rate that this will protect them from any complaints against them.[26]

Complementing the trend in tactics and use of the courts has been the push for greater police powers. One step in this process—of great significance for the mainland Irish—was the passage of the Prevention of Terrorism Act. Rushed through parliament in a day after the Birmingham bombings, it had in fact been in preparation for some time. Under its provisions the state took powers to deport UK citizens from one part of the country to another and the police got the right to hold suspects for seven days. Brian Rose-Smith has clearly shown that the PTA has contributed little to unearthing Republican active service units, but much to destroying legal political activity opposed to Britain's presence in Ireland.[27] The PTA has also been used in textbook counter-insurgency fashion to intimidate whole Irish communities. Following the Airey Neave killing, for example, the Irish areas of North London were saturated by police who took to:

> Staking out certain houses and grabbing anyone going in or out; sitting openly in cars outside homes, pubs and clubs; and even going into church clubs, the music clubs, the Irish ballrooms . . . a whole community has been under intense observation. The Irish are experiencing what blacks in the cities term the 'sus offensive'.[28]

The deliberations of the Royal Commission on Criminal Procedure—set up in 1977—have been accompanied by a concerted police campaign for further powers. McNee, the Metropolitan Police Chief, argued in his memorandum for a general power to hold suspects for 72 hours before charging, with the option of a further 72 hours on the agreement of a single magistrate. Other demands included an end to the right to silence during interrogation, abolition of cautionings, a general power to set up roadblocks and compulsorily fingerprint whole communities. This is just the shortlist of a series of demands which have been echoed by other senior policemen.

A pointer to the sort of powers likely to be acceded to in England and Wales is contained in the Criminal Justice (Scotland) Bill 1980. Under its provisions police in Scotland will be able to detain people without charge on the streets for as long as they deem necessary, to hold suspects for six hours without access to lawyers or informing relatives, and forcibly bodysearch and fingerprint. All the new powers will be exercisable without formal arrest, caution or charge. Alderson, Chief Constable of Devon and Cornwall, has described these powers as 'akin to those of an occupying army'.

Confronting and controlling mass action

As we argued earlier, one of the major influences on the growing shift to coercion during the seventies was militant action on the part of organised workers during the early years of the decade. By 1972 the elite among both military and police strategists were already engaged in a major debate as to how best to respond to the challenge of mass and flying pickets. The previous year Brigadier Kitson, drawing on long experience of colonial counter-insurgency operations, had already argued in his book *Low Intensity Operations* that the army should have a greatly increased role in suppressing internal dissent. But there were others amongst the establishment who recognised that such a step taken outside a period of revolutionary crisis was likely to be counterproductive. They could point to the fact that one hundred and fifty years ago internal use of the army had had the effect of driving working class people to detest and hate the ultimate power of the state and support agitation against it. Because of this, use of the army for public order purposes had been phased out as police forces were formed from the ranks of the working class. Their authority was that much more effective precisely because it did not rest on the overt use of muskets and sabres but, as one of the first commissioners of the Metropolitan Police observed, 'upon public approval of their existence, actions and behaviour, and their ability to secure and maintain public respect.'[29] How to move into a position of greater strength vis-á-vis mass action without jeopardising this consent to the rule of law and the authority of the state was a major problem for the government of the time.

The resolution of the debate led to a covert restructuring of the police force and its relations to the army in order to plug the gaps the working class offensive had revealed. Thus the cabinet committee set up in the aftermath of the 1972 miners' strike fixed on a strategy designed 'to encourage a convergence of the army and police role ... the result of this new approach is that the government has greatly increased its capacity for a flexible response if there is any threat to the security of the state.'[30] In the years following the fall of the Heath government the Labour administration managed to stabilise relations with the industrial working class by co-opting the leadership of the labour movement via the social contract and, in exchange for wage restraint, bringing in new legislation extending rights of working class organisation. The restructuring of the security forces (the front line of the police and the reserve of the army) continued during this period with the updating of operational plans for army units on the mainland, the formation of new police specialist squads, a marked increase in police weapons training and joint exercises between the army and police. In addition the period saw increasing special branch surveillance of potential dissidents, especially militant trade unionists, and the introduction of new methods of riot control.

All these trends have been fully documented elsewhere.[31] Here we want to stress the way in which the divisions between the surplus population and the industrial working class have provided the state apparatus with opportunities for both gaining practical experience and acclimatising the public to the use of far tougher methods at points of contested authority. In 1977 Lewisham provided a very clear example of the way in which such tactics have been first-blooded in the conflict with the black communities. First horses and truncheons were used brutally and with far less warning than in the past in order to clear a route through an anti-fascist crowd for the National Front. By deliberately doing this the police provoked a conflict which then became the occasion for introducing 'two imports from Northern Ireland—snatch squads employed throughout the demonstration and riot shields.'[32]

Operating from behind these shields were officers of the Metropolitan Special Patrol Group. Initially set up in 1965, the SPG has become steadily more prominent over the last decade and every major British police force now has a similar para-military force, trained in all the latest riot control techniques and heavily equipped with firearms. Their role, equipment and tactics are closely modelled on the Special Weapons and Tactics Squads set up in the USA following the disorders of the sixties. Like their British counterparts, SWAT squads 'require military-style teamwork and policemen are usually trained to function as individuals with discretionary powers'.[33] In Britain riot training is now given to police both through a standard course and by rotating personnel through the SPG-type units. A similar trend is evident in arms training and 'the claim that the British police remains substantially an unarmed force, the only one in the world, is largely a semantic quibble . . . for good or ill, in all those cases where it matters, the British police are now in effect an armed and fully equipped technical force.'[34]

SPG-type units have used their flying-wedge tactics to break up mass pickets in unionisation disputes from Grunwicks in 1977 to the *Nottingham Post* in 1979. They made up the snatch squads at Lewisham and were used to bludgeon anti-fascists off the streets of

Southall. That operation lead to the death of Blair Peach, and renewed outcries about SPG brutality which were reinforced when it was subsequently revealed that officers were in possession of unauthorised weapons and that one had a predilection for Nazi regalia. Brutal as individuals the SPG may be, but their baton charges on the streets of Southall issued from the standard procedure security forces are trained to follow when confronting a riot. The authors of the *Technology of Political Control* have laid out the task of forces in such a situation: 'to stop the 'contagion' from spreading out of control, prevent reinforcements from reaching the demonstrators and destroy the crowd as a purposeful entity.'[35] Baton charges, carrying the risk of death and serious injury, are an essential tool for this operation in the Britain of the 1980s. After the police had closed ranks in a cover up, a coroners court, in concluding that Blair Peach met his death by 'misadventure', clearly signalled that people daring to participate in mass protest would just have to accept death as a possible consequence.

In the aftermath of the Bristol riot both the Home Secretary and various police chiefs have called for expansion of existing 'order squads' and floated the proposition of setting up a stand-by force capable of dealing with 'national emergencies or problems'. Once again confrontation with groups in the surplus population has provided the cue for further restructuring of the type which has so far made use of the army in a public order role unnecessary. Nevertheless the seventies did see the army used in a strike-breaking role in the public sector and some of its units are known to undertake exercises in which they fire at crowds in a mainland city after the police have lost control.

The state response to mass action in the seventies has in the main been organisational and operational rather than legislative. This has issued from a recognition that a direct outlawing of peaceful protest runs the risk of encouraging more militant forms of action. Whatever the quantitative problems of policing hundreds of marches a year on the streets of the mainland cities, the price is quite clearly worth paying for its safety-valve value in a bourgeois democracy. Nevertheless in the current period it has become necessary for the state to achieve a greater degree of control over such manifestations of discontent and the review of public order currently being carried out will almost certainly lead to restrictive legislation; it also proved necessary to legislate earlier in the seventies in order to both discourage and take sanctions against the growing use of the occupation tactic by trade unionists and community activists. In both these areas of the law the split between the main body of the working class and other groups has provided opportunities for the state to act. Following on from a large number of factory occupations between 1970 and 1974, the Law Commission produced a report which proposed outlawing occupations outright by making trespass a criminal offence—it was at that time wholly a civil matter. This proposal posed a direct threat both to trade unionists and to a large number of squatters who had occupied empty property in the cities. The latter soon became the target of a press campaign which sought to justify the proposals by creating 'unsubstantiated fears that anyone who left their home for more than five minutes would find it squatted by homeless people'.[36]

So gross was the media's disregard for the facts that its efforts can only be seen as having been an attempt to create a panic in the working class that the home—the last sanctuary of personal life—was under seige. Many squatting activists, aware of the rift between most squatters and the respectable working class, attempted to bridge it. Such a political orientation laid the basis for a number of local victories over housing issues, but squatters alone were unable to block the state's determination to take the tactic of occupation out of the repertoire of legitimate working class action. In the event, the new law has provided a far less inflexible instrument than a total ban, which could have led to mass arrests by imposing a duty on the police to intervene in all occupations however harmless or transitory. The final form of the legislation allows much leeway to the police over the question of making arrests for certain categories of ill-defined behaviour that may be committed in the course of an occupation. Largely because occupation as a tactic is an ineffective one in the face of outright closure, the number of factory occupations has been relatively small since the passage of the law. It remains in the locker, though, for use in future emergencies and arguably has already had a deterrent effect.

If squatters provided convenient scapegoats as regards the trespass law, the National Front has played a crucial role as provocateur in the field of controlling mass protest. Through its covert attacks on black and left-wing targets and its stridently overt exercising of 'democratic' freedoms under police protection, the organisation has remained true to a classic fascist pedigree. As Gramsci saw it, the task of such groups is 'to make use of illegal means, while the state appears to remain within legality, and thus to re-organise the state itself.'[37]

We have already mentioned the way in which NF provocations have provided occasion for tactical and strategic innovations on the part of the police. At Southall they played a similar role in the legislative field as the events there led to a review of the 1936 Public Order Act under the aegis of the incoming Tory government. Innovations now under consideration include a general statutory power for the police to require a crowd to disperse if they anticipate violence (this is modelled on Section 24 of the Northern Ireland (Emergency Provisions) Act 1978), a power to dictate the route of marches, and the possible extension of such controls to rallies and meetings. Alderson, Chief Constable of Devon and Cornwall, has gone further in arguing that marches could be banned and protest confined to rallying in set places on the grounds that 'the funds saved in this way could be re-allocated to housing the homeless and other pressing needs'![38]

It is clear that the state is seeking to acquire a far tighter rein over public demonstration and that current proposals would be a significant blow to the effective organisation of protest. These moves issue directly out of the NF's role as provocateur and have somewhat naively been reinforced by elements in the labour movement and anti-fascist camp. Thus it was the left at the 1977 Labour Party Conference who successfully proposed a motion calling for the Home Secretary to be given banning powers. Such demands completely overlook the relationship between fascist activities and state reorganisation. They have contributed to a climate in which it is possible for a right-wing Tory government to present repressive changes in the law as merely a logical response to logistical problems. It should go without saying that powers of this type are far more likely to be used against the left and organised workers during the next decade than they are against the right.

Opposing the drive for an authoritarian consensus

The gearing up of the forces of law and order for the tasks of maintaining social control over marginalised individuals, quelling spontaneous disorder and containing organised protest does not preclude attempts to rebuild consent in the inner city. Nor does it mean that the British police are going to take on the public guise of such paramilitary forces as the French CRS. Quite the contrary—they will continue striving to retain a benevolent reputation—launching furious assaults against whoever dents it, be they liberal journalists, elected authorities or the clergy.[39] They will work hard to integrate technological change into the helpful bobby image—thus when the mass picketing at Grunwicks demonstrated design faults in the traditional helmet 'an improved model, outwardly similar in appearance, but with a special protective lining and a more effective quick release strap was taken into experimental use soon afterwards'.[40] On the ideological front, as in the immediate past, they and their allies will also seize on every pretext to reforge a new and more authoritarian consensus in society—so that the use of increasingly coercive tactics will still rest on a bedrock of popular approval. Crucial to this task is a constant stirring of 'respectable working class' anxieties and a playing up of divisions that already exist in the working class.

As we have seen, local working class communities in urban Britain have been subjected to strong winds of change in the postwar period. Members of these communities no longer have the solidarity of kith and kin to help them weather times of crisis. Instead individuals today face the piecemeal dismembering of their culture and their social organisation in relative isolation. Calls for law and order at a time like this can elicit very strong responses from a beleaguered respectable working class because rising crime coincides with these other experiences of collapsing patterns of social organisation and economic uncertainty. The criminal, unknown, violent, coming from the dark, can easily become the embodiment of all these disturbing experiences. Furthermore rising crime does pose a very real threat to the possessions and comforts painfully accumulated over many years of labour. By the early seventies sections of the white working class had experienced sufficient social and economic dislocation to respond positively to campaigns of social anxiety and moral panic which were to be hung around the necks of a few key figures.

The spotlight has focused repeatedly on the immigrant —swamping, in Thatcher's words, our great British culture. Through the immigration laws blacks have been openly portrayed as a problem and, more covertly, through a host of cultural vehicles, as a major cause of the disintegration of working class culture. In addition the old racist myths of black savagery have been given a modern currency within the last decade, as state functionaries and media have co-operated in promoting two prolonged waves of moral panic about 'mugging'. This is an imported American term for robbery with some degree of violence which captures the transatlantic urban crisis in a sensationalised image. An old crime with a new name, it came into prominence in 1972 as street crime committed by black youth 'began to receive a great deal of coverage in the press in the form of crime reports, features, editorials, statements by representatives of the police, judges, the Home Secretary, politicians and various public spokesmen'.[41]

The authors of *Policing the Crisis* have shown that police 'mugging statistics' were not only highly questionable but that they do not bear out the repeated assertions about there being an epidemic of this crime. Following on from this they suggest that these moral panics originated from the shared, ill-founded anxieties of those working in the state control apparatus. We would put more stress on the way in which they formed part of an attempt to pin a general criminal stigma on the revolt of West Indian youth in all its forms and at the same time divide the generations within the West Indian communities. In a similar way campaigns concerning the savage terrorist and the trade union wrecker prepared to intimidate, have seen the creation of folk-devils in a way which not only distorts reality but also corresponds to the real and distinct threats posed to state control in arenas where consent has foundered.

At the forefront of recent moves to both strengthen the state apparatus and secure public approval for tougher methods have been a group of prominent senior policemen abetted by the Police Federation and the Tory Party. The emergence of senior police-men in this role was facilitated by the 1964 Police Act which abolished the flimsy democratic controls previously exercised by local watch committees, ensured that no-one now has the power to give police chiefs orders and reduced their accountability to any elected body to the mere duty to produce an annual report for perusal by local police authorities; (in the case of the Metropolitan Commissioner the report goes to the Home Secretary). The recommendation of the Royal Commission that led to the 1964 Police Act also set in motion a long-term reduction in the number of police forces, and the combination of the two has produced, in Sir Robert Mark's gleeful words, 'all the benefits of a national police force with none of the disadvantages . . . they have never before been so free from interference in their operational role'.[42]

Prominent individual police chiefs have tended to con-centrate in their pronouncements on different aspects of 'the law and order crisis', variously stressing the breakdown of traditional morality (Anderton), the industrial/political dimension (Oxford/McNee), the threat of big time crime (Mark), etc. They have all at various times made attacks on specific legislation (e.g. the Bail Act) endorsed calls for greater powers (of detention, for example), attacked critics of police methods, and made wider organisational demands and policy pronouncements. Together, they constitute a lobby that is now prepared to attack anything that smacks of liberalism.

Some responses to the shift towards coercion in the state's activities have tended to be informed by a nostalgic view that Britain is a model liberal democracy, whose constitution and state form can be effectively used against the inroads of the law and order brigade in the current period. Thus increased coercion is often met by reasoned attempts to persuade police and state functionaries that they are not acting in their own best interests when they alienate so many people; inquests have been approached in the expectation that the state apparatus can be effectively used to control the excesses of its own shock troops; and calls for state controlled inquiries have followed from police handling of organised protest and spontaneous disorders.

In our view the assessment that Britain is a liberal democracy is profoundly wrong and a strategy which relies on seeking to utilise and defend what exists will be counter-productive. Britain has for a long time been one of the least democratic of the central capitalist states: there is no democratic element in the selection of a judiciary who have unrivalled powers to reinterpret the law; the police force cannot be externally investigated and its operations are subject to no effective external authority; the state itself is protected by the most all embracing and powerful secrecy laws in the West. Holding on to the mirage of Britain as a liberal democracy has the effect of militating against the evolution of an effective strategy to combat the shift towards coercion, by ceding much of the battleground to McNee and his ilk. For it is their argument that Britain is too liberal for the protection of the ordinary citizen. Within its terms, every additional insecurity the working class has to face becomes the justification for increasing the power of the coercive apparatus.

Evolving an effective socialist strategy in response to current developments is no easy task. It requires a break with the whole framework which sees the state apparatus as potentially benign and the mounting of a counter attack on a broad front. This would counterpose calls for greater police powers and the increased use of coercion with relentless exposure of abuse of power and corruption, the roots of 'crime' and the class composition and interests of the judiciary. It would need to build on recent examples of independent public inquiries into police operations and seek to broaden their focus so that the operations of the law and order apparatus are subjected to the widest possible independent working class scrutiny. Exposing the underlying causes of the shift to coercion and demonstrating the inability of the state to provide security for the working class would be a necessary part of this. Such a strategy would also need to be drawn up with the clear aim of building unity between those groups whose isolation has facilitated the shift to coercion. And it would need to recognise that the issue is fast becoming one of whether the state will be able to seal off those arenas in which consent to its authority is withering and impose a more exacting discipline, or whether new forms of social authority—counterposed to those of the state—will be able to begin to develop.

During the early seventies the no-go areas of Catholic Belfast and Derry saw the growth of the most fully developed organs of working class authority to be seen in these islands since the General Strike. On the mainland, in the latter part of the decade, embryonic forms of these organs have already emerged with the beginnings of self-defence organisations in the Afro-Caribbean and Asian communities. Whether such self-defence organisations can broaden their political support or effectively ward off repression by becoming more permanent remains very much an open question.

New Unities and Alliances

In Chapter 2 we argued that the nature of the capitalist mode of production is such that it precludes a smooth and peaceful transition from prolonged stagnation to long-term growth. In the late nineteenth century the crisis was resolved through a dramatic widening of the world market as the colonies were subjugated and integrated into a global system of production. In the inter-war period, however, this avenue of expansion was no longer available, and the resolution to economic stagnation and falling profitability eventually emerged out of a series of crushing defeats of the working class. Given the structure of the world market, there are reasons for believing that growth within a capitalist framework can only be resumed in Britain today through the effects of the kind of defeats which occurred then. Such major shifts in the balance of class forces can be achieved either through the cumulative effects of many small defeats, the erosion of civil liberties and growing demoralisation within the labour movement, or through major contestations of civil power. The Thatcher government has embarked on the former course. However, because of the great defensive and institutionalised strength of the British working class, it is difficult to see how such a long-term shift in the balance of class forces can be brought about gradually—and, to quote Brookings again, 'one needs an optimistic disposition to suppose that a democratic political system can eliminate the problem'. It may well be that within the next decade we will have to face a major attempt to solve the 'problem of trade union power' for a prolonged period. Whether such a confrontation occurs or not will probably be determined by the success or failure of current attempts gradually to undermine organised labour. Whichever is the case, building unity between diverse sections of the working class is now more urgent than at any time in the post war period.

The present government is not approaching the task of recreating the conditions for profitable expansion in the same way as the last Conservative government. The fall of the Heath government is still fresh in its mind. Rather than rely on the power of parliament to discipline the working class—as that administration did— it has pursued fiscal and monetary policies which have as their central, if disguised, objective the unleashing of more impersonal market forces in such a way as to promote mass unemployment. As Peter Jenkins, the *Guardian*'s eminently right-of-centre commentator put it in July 1980:

> the government's policies are deepening the manufacturing recession and will go on doing so. The recession is not a mistake, it is not a natural disaster like a Wimbledon cloudburst—it is an instrument of government policy.

Some of the short-term benefits of using very high levels of unemployment as an instrument to control wage bargaining have already become evident. Wage settlements in the West Midlands area, for example, were running at 8 per cent in the engineering industry during the summer of 1980 at a time when inflation was over 20 per cent. In the longer-term mass unemployment introduces fear and insecurity into workforces, individualises consciousness and further deepens the already deep divides inside the working class, between men and women, old and young, black and white; between those in and out of work, those in the most and those in the least prosperous regions, those at the top of the hierarchy of labour and those at the bottom.

The divisive thrust by the new Thatcherite bloc is one of the most noticeable and frightening of its activities. While the mass media focuses anxiety on 'subversives', 'scroungers' and 'deviants', and Thatcher's lieutenants serve up a sickly stew of traditional morality aimed at reintroducing the elements of patriotism, discipline and motherhood back into the national culture, the divides are systematically widened. Cuts are made in the level of welfare benefits; there is talk of the unemployed having to do voluntary work in order to draw the dole; child benefits are allowed to fall behind inflation, restrictions are placed on young workers' rights and on maternity leave provisions; the Employment Act contains clauses which will have a differentially severe impact on many women workers; immigration procedures have been tightened up even further. Moreover the whole movement of this society in crisis places its burdens and oppressions in a hundred everyday ways more heavily on those groups so heavily represented in the surplus population and singled out for special attention by this government.

The problem of working class unity is particularly acute in the inner cities where growing fractions of the working class have no entry to the basic defensive institutions of the working class—the trade unions. These include the unemployed, the casually employed, homeworkers, the long-term sick, the old and those looking after children full-time. As we have seen, these people make up a substantial portion of the population in the working class quarters of the great cities, and even a majority in some areas. The bastions of trade union organisation in manufacturing industry have been particularly weakened by the wholesale closure of large scale industry, while many of the post-war growth points of employment, especially in the service sector have proved hard to organise. Employers have been aware for some time of these great difficulties facing organisation, and in London alone for example there have been a significant number of disputes over union recognition in the last few years: Grunwicks, Garners, Futters, Spiralynx, The Economist Bookshop and Chix. The government's enterprise zones are based on the recognition that the special attractions of inner cities for investment lies in the possibility of using cheap unorganised labour.

All this points to the importance of trade union membership and organisation drives, along with struggles over working conditions and health and safety questions in the sweatshop belts and the leisure and entertainment industries. And the fact that socialists are having to confront basic issues of working class organisation once again illustrates how any grander strategy has first to come to terms with the changes in the composition and distribution of the class which have occurred over the post-war period.

Alongside the weakness of trade union organisation in the older urban areas there is the further problem of the absence of mass-based organisations capable of giving unified expression to the political needs of the working class. The Labour Party has held on to some of its links with the urban working class through its periodic bouts of electoral activity. But the many other ways it was organically integrated into a working class culture, when it actually was a live mass party, have withered away. In many working class areas the party organisation is an empty shell—and where it is still a viable organisation its active membership is all too often exclusively white in colour and white collar in composition. Where Labour is in charge of a local authority, it is either seen as part of a local bureaucratic and alien elite, or where its rule is unchallenged, as irretrievably self-serving and corrupt. Even in those authorities, such as Lambeth for example, where a vigorous left Labour leadership has come to power, there has been little in the way of transformation of the relations between the party and the local working class. The party activists, despite the council's policy of equal opportunity for blacks, have remained overwhelmingly white, skilled and non-manual in occupation in stark contrast to the black manual workers who make up a quarter of Lambeth's population.

In the face of the Tory onslaught on public expenditure Lambeth and other similar councils have had to raise local rates sharply in order to preserve as many services as possible from the axe. In doing so they have run the danger of further alienating local people at a time when attempting to ameliorate the problems of the inner city brings one slap up against laws eroding the freedom of action of local government, the power of the financial institutions and the whole movement of a capitalist economy in profound crisis.

During the 1974–79 Labour government many inner city authorities indulged in a great deal of special pleading for greater powers of intervention and an increase in their share of state spending so that the effects of economic decline could be countered—in doing so they reinforced the illusion that state intervention along the lines of regional policies that have already failed could solve the problems of these areas. The left wing of the Labour Party is as trapped within this conception of socialist advance through the growth of the state as the centre of the party. Indeed, in many ways it is more attached to this political strategy than the leadership. In the spheres which are the particular concern of this book—the uneven development of the capitalist mode of production in space and time—Labour's left wing has mapped out a programme of action, under the title of the Alternative Economic Strategy (AES). It has appeared in a number of variants but its main proposals can be summarised as follows: the government should respond to the crisis by stimulating expansion, increasing public spending and ending monetarist policies. A rigid system of price controls would contain inflation, while import controls would ensure that expanded demand does not simply suck in imports. The state would gain real power to increase productive investment in two ways—through an extension of public ownership into all the major industrial and financial sectors and through planning agreements with the big privately owned corporations. Companies will be induced to be socially responsible in their investment plans by an extension of 'industrial democracy' along with planning agreements.

The 'Alternative' strategy has been developed in response to the evident unwillingness of British capital to invest sufficiently in the UK to maintain the UK's position in the international league of industrial nations. Its cornerstone is an analysis, most clearly articulated by Stuart Holland[1], that the basic root of the problem lies in the rise of the transnationals. These have upset the mechanisms of demand management to the point where a nation state can no longer control the economy. This means that a government must now involve itself directly in production with the aim of counterbalancing transnational power in order to force these companies to plan, invest and produce according to social needs as determined by the state. Both Holland and more radical supporters of the AES recognise the need to mobilise the working class outside parliament in the event of the right obstructing these policies.

While we do not have the space to fully review the debates about AES and its theoretical underpinnings we do wish to make a few brief points.[2] One of the virtues of the AES is that it provides a plan which may be able to convince some sections of the working class that there is another way of weathering the storm apart from allowing market forces their freedom. As such it can do more than abstract calls for confrontation in helping to stem the demoralisation engendered by the crisis. Nevertheless, advancing along its lines would not merely be inadequate, but would carry with it grave dangers if attempted without the prior creation of new alliances and unities within the working class.

Within the AES perspective capitalism is viewed as an essentially progressive system whose irregularities and faults can be smoothed out by a state apparatus with sufficient economic power to gently but firmly discipline the major capitalist groupings. Thus the mixed economy is to survive, and the transnationals will find their dynamism harnessed for national and regional development. The basic flaw in this strategy is that the transnationals' 'dynamism' arises from their ability to reap maximum profits through exploitation of uneven development on a world scale. Any company prevented from pursuing these above average profits is liable to founder under the blows of competition from other enterprises which are not subject to such constraints. Moreover companies nationalised by the government would, if they were to be a competitive force, have to operate in just as ruthlessly efficient a way (in terms of maximising profits) as the other leading firms. Working conditions and wages would not necessarily improve, nor would the general features of alienated labour under capital's rule disappear, just because the state had taken over ownership of a particular enterprise. Indeed unless there was substantial improvement in working conditions in these firms, it would be hard to rally even the organised working class to the defence of this programme once the attacks on it began.

The programme would also place legal restrictions on the free movement of capital, in the form of rigorous exchange controls and compulsory planning agreements. But capital mobility, as we have argued earlier, is the very life blood of the capitalist mode of production. Without complete control over the movement of capital—between firms, sectors, regions and countries—capitalists cannot be assured of reaping higher than average profits and so surviving the competitive struggle between individual capitals. Thus the Alternative Economic Strategy falls between two stools—it does not go far enough down the road to reverse the consequences of recession and restructuring and so be assured of the militant support of the majority of the working class. But it places sufficient restrictions on capital mobility as to be assured of the ferocious opposition of the established order.

This brings us perhaps to the greatest weakness in the AES—its reliance on parliament and the state machinery for socialist advance. A left Labour government committed to this strategy would meet opposition to its legislation from the media, the upper echelons of the civil service, the right wing of its own party along with the other parties in parliament, and the interlocking nexus of professional organisations, the judiciary, and business organisations. On the evidence of Britain's own past (the 1948 steel nationalisation, the 1966 devaluation and the attempts to implement elements of Labour's 1974 industrial programme) and on the evidence of other countries where similar programmes have been put forward (such as in Chile) the opposition would take the form of boycotts of the new state bodies, investment strikes, a flight of capital abroad, the refusal of foreign loans, the orchestration of a balance of payments crisis, and even outright sabotage of existing plant and machinery. Such moves would be designed to force the government to capitulate or to create such economic and social chaos through shortages, inflation and rising unemployment as to deprive the government of its popular base. Against these forces, entrenched in the dominant institutions, such a government would require an immeasurably greater social force than 'respect for the law' by the established order and the actions of a state bureaucracy committed at its top layers to the rule of capital. Without a sustained and developing mass working class movement behind such a left government it would simply have no social power to enforce its legislation.

Although some proponents of the AES recognise this principle there are grave problems in the relationship which has been established between the organisations and institutions of the working class on the one hand and this programme on the other, which will impede such a mobilisation. During the five years of Labour's last administration, Tony Benn, the most publicly prominent advocate of the AES remained silent while the government cut the level of real wages, axed social spending, and presided over the greatest increase in unemployment for over thirty years. Many of those in the Labour party who have championed and developed the programme have spent little political energy in supporting workers' struggles or coming to terms with the divides inside the class—many of which were deepened by the last Labour government.

Those in the machinery of state, be it local or national cannot escape the constraints which come with a position of power in a class divided society. The most central of these restrictions is the impossibility of using a state apparatus, which embodies the interests of the dominant class in society, as the main instrument for fundamentally attacking the position of that class. The simple resolve of left labour politicians to summon up, from their ministerial offices, a working class movement when they run into trouble solves nothing, for it ignores the many reasons why they will be unable to effectively carry out such a mobilisation.

Moreover the AES has in no sense grown out of the resistance to oppression developed by working class people over the last decade. It remains a programme evolved through academic work, debate at Transport House and annual conferences. While a national strategy to resolve the crisis to the benefit of the working class remains vitally important, it is our contention that a strategy which can be implemented can only evolve in relation to the everyday struggles of working people and with close regard to the divisions inside the working class. Marx put programmes, like the AES, in perspective when he wrote: 'Every step of real movement is more important than a dozen programmes.'[3] We would argue that the fragmented nature of the working class requires activity now as well as programmatic preparations for a future Labour government. And with the Tories using mass unemployment as the basic regulator of class relations, it is vitally important that the labour movement take the organisation of the unemployed seriously. The fight for a thirty-five hour working week, for job sharing with no loss of pay, for the ending of overtime, and for workers control of the introduction of new technology, are all obviously important goals to be fought for within the labour movement. But they are not enough to achieve unity between sections of the surplus population and the organised working class. So far marches to the annual TUC, Tory and Labour Party conferences have made up the bulk of the left's work with the unemployed. There have been recent suggestions that the established unions should start recruiting unemployed members. But the thrust of our analysis is that we must now build permanent organisations of the unemployed, with substantial resources from the trade unions, as integral parts of the labour movement. It is no longer adequate to treat the unemployed as fodder for a propaganda campaign against an incumbent government. The extent and duration of the recession is far too serious for that kind of approach. The de-indexing of benefits and the floating of proposals to make dole payments conditional on voluntary work mark the beginnings of an assault similar to that the unemployed suffered in the thirties. They open up possibilities of new defensive organisations—but we must beware of transposing the forms, tactics and organisations of the inter war period to today as if the working class had remained unchanged throughout the post war period. The organisations of the thirties were effective precisely because they grew out of working class culture as it existed then; organising with the unemployed to-day can only be done on the same basis.

The second area for action concerns the necessity to address divisions between the producers and consumers of public services. This is particularly important in the older working class areas where public sector workers along with those who are heavily dependant on their services make up a substantial proportion of the population.

The events of the 'winter of discontent' show the results of ignoring those divisions. On that occasion, public sector workers, seeking to break through the pay policy, withdrew services to the public. Hardship to the consumers then followed. The media and senior state managers jumped in to turn the population against the providers of services. The dispute ended unsatisfactorily for the public sector unions once the divide between provider and consumer had been successfully prised apart. As the process of the cuts feeds down to affect manning levels, and produce redundancies, we can expect more of such confrontations. And if the unions are going to effectively challenge government policy they are going to have to rely on more than abstract calls to working class solidarity, or the natural justice of their pay claims. The sectionalism of the British working class has laid the ground for its own defeat unless it can forge new alliances and unities. In the public sector, an alliance between public sector workers and the consumers of services is needed; but such an alliance can only come about through dismantling the barriers that prevent workers and consumers having any control over the services produced and received. Such an alliance would open up the institutions of the welfare state to inspection, would ask what are the health, education, welfare, etc. needs of localities and how these needs can be met from existing resources.[4] In the political climate of 1981 onwards, militant defensive struggles to protect the status quo will invariably fail. And the creation of alliances will have to involve a real response to the apathy and hostility many working class people feel towards the institutions of the welfare state.

A strategy which stresses building alliances between consumers and producers and between different groups within the working class, requires that the particular problems and oppressions of those groups be taken seriously. It is at least in part because the social structure of British capitalism is so thoroughly imbued with racial and sexual subordination, that autonomous black and women's organisations have developed to articulate and oppose those oppressions. Moreover, it is only through the growing power of these movements that those groups at the top of the hierarchy of labour—the white skilled male working class—are coming to understand that these subordinations are an integral part of wage labourers' own oppression. These movements have developed a richness of political action, and a depth of analysis which is all too often missing from the economistic approaches of the labour movement.

When unity has been achieved between these movements (or groups in the surplus population which go to form them) and the labour movement, the results have been very powerful; in different ways Grunwicks, the Anti-Nazi League Carnivals, and the mobilisations which kept the anti-abortion Corrie bill off the statute book, all showed the dynamism of such alliances. As we outlined in the last chapter, with the shift towards the pole of coercion in the state apparatus accelerating, wider and wider groups in the population have begun to experience the state in new and disturbing ways. In this situation, the knowledge, tactics and strategies built up inside the black communities and the surplus population will be of great use to those entering into collective struggle. The fruits of over a decade of feminist and black political struggle will only be generalised, however, if a vigorous confrontation takes place with the racist and patriarchal attitudes which permeate the working class.

The success of the right here in the UK, and elsewhere in the West, indicates the extent to which mainstream socialist politics have become discredited. We have argued that a major source of this lack of popular support is the labour movement's reliance on state solutions to the problems and oppressions of everyday life. The Thatcherite assertion that health can only return to the body politic through each individual and every institution braving the storms of free enterprise on their own two feet has gained ground against the tired old labourist responses. The right has offered a radical solution to the crisis—albeit one that is based on exploiting the individual's reactionary responses to it and latching on to the 'morbid symptoms' thrown up by it. The left has ignored this field; the social democrats placing their faith in greater and greater doses of bureaucratic state medicine while the far left is trapped within the terrain of militant defensive postures and party building. But we can no longer rely simply on the self evident truths of socialism if we are to roll back the right wing offensive. We have also to contest the ground of the personal which the right has recently monopolised.

As we showed in Chapter 6, the hegemony of the state is, in part, reproduced through its welfare organs latching onto 'personal problems', distorting their causes and offering bureaucratised palliatives and solutions. The state, in short, has an extensive personal political practice, and it is one which has largely gone unchallenged by socialists. The lack of acknowledgement by the left of individual's personal responses to the all pervasive social crisis has disarmed it, in the face of a right wing populist assault. But socialists are now faced with opportunities which can best be seized if they realise the extent to which the personal is political.

The withdrawal of state services from working class areas is a cleft in the state's flank the left cannot afford to ignore. As the government begins to cut back on the whole range of social services the question will be—who will fill the vacuum? The right and conservative church forces in alliance with the state, or the labour movement in alliance with progressive bodies. One thing is certain, the time when socialists could launch projects which were financed by the state is over. And we would question the traditional view that insists that the state pay for the services or they will not be provided. Such a view seems imbued with social democratic notions of the beneficient nature of the state. Against this notion we would pose the concept of the independence of the working class, not only in trade union terms, but also in the broader fields of welfare and education. With the development of local resource centres, unemployed workers' centres, co-operative enterprises, organised childcare networks, such ideas are beginning to take shape on the ground. Rather than view these suspiciously, we think they should be extended; in fact it is probably only through their extension that socialists will come to have any influence within the surplus population. Political activity in the inner city has, for some time, been able to utilise community organisations buoyed up by state handouts; but in the 1980's either it will be materially supported by the organised working class and grow out of that class's struggle in all its dimensions—including the so-called personal—or it will fold.

The expansion of the surplus population holds both negative and positive possibilities for socialists. The divisions which exist within the whole class penetrate the surplus population but here there are no unitary structures (such as party or trade union organisation) to bind it together. Most of its members are united by their alienation from Labourism, which fails to take up the basis of their oppression; but it is not politically homogenous —having British Movement youth at one pole and radicalised Asian youth at the other. The demise of the present government might well see an explosion of neo-fascist politics from their base in the surplus population. The role of the fascist groups decreased during the first year of Thatcher's government—however it would be a mistake to think that this form of racist populism is a dying creed. Thatcher's policies have both nurtured it and at the same time masked it. There may well be ugly times ahead. But in addition to struggling against these dangers we need to exploit the opportunities the present situation holds out to us. The political activity we have outlined—around permanent organisations of the unemployed, the consumer-producer public sector alliance, and exploiting the clefts in the state's welfare flank, would, we believe, be a start in that direction. They would both unite sections of the surplus population with the main body of the class and at the same time create the possibility of the distinct groups within the working class addressing and recognising each other's distinctive political needs.

We have tried in this book to make a particular contribution to socialist thinking; to put together one more section of the jigsaw. We have looked at what is actually happening in the big conurbations, to demystify the process of industrial change, to glance into the windows of family life. We have held on to two basic ideas in doing this. Firstly, that we are currently living through a long wave of stagnation which can only be ended within capitalism by an erosion of our hard-won rights and freedoms, and through increased exploitation and repression. Secondly, that divisions within the working class are of crucial significance in the established order's attempts to reimpose their domination through inflicting major defeats on the working class. It is a stark picture—and no less so because each day which passes seems to confirm its accuracy. But it is also one that contains within it suggestions for a way out of the impasse that socialist organisation and the labour movement is now in—through the struggle to create new alliances and new unities.

References

Introduction pages 7–26

1. Mayhew, *London Labour and London Poor*, Vol. 2, 1861, pp. 322–23 and G. Stedman Jones, *Outcast London: A Study in the Relationship of Classes in Victorian Society*, Harmondsworth: Penguin 1976, p. 53.
2. See G. Stedman Jones *op. cit.* Chapter 16.
3. Franklin, *From the Movement* New York: Van Nostrand Reinhold 1971, p. 13.
4. For material on the North American developments outlined here, see Piven and Cloward, *Regulating the Poor*, London: Tavistock 1972; Piven and Cloward (eds) *The Politics of Turmoil*, New York: Vintage 1975; Alcaly and Mermelstein, *The Fiscal Crisis of American Cities*, New York: Vintage 1976.
5. C.D.P., *Gilding the Ghetto: the State and Poverty Experiments*, pp. 9–10.
6. C.D.P. *op. cit.*
7. *Inner Area Studies: Summary of Final Reports*, HMSO 1977.
8. K. Marx, *Capital*, Vol. 1, Harmondsworth: Penguin 1976, p. 794.
9. K. Marx *op. cit.* pp. 781–802.
10. J. Stevenson and C. Cook, *The Slump: Society and Politics During the Depression*, London: Quartet 1979, p. 59.
11. Marx and Engels, *Manifesto of the Communist Party*, in *Selected Works*, Moscow: Progress Publishers 1968.

1. A Long Phase of Stagnation pages 27–45

1. Glyn and Sutcliffe, *British Capitalism, Workers and the Profits Squeeze,* Harmondsworth: Penguin 1972, table 3.3., p. 66.
2. E. Mandel, *The Second Slump*, London: New Left Books 1978, table 5, p. 22.
3. Glyn and Harrison, *The British Economic Disaster*, London: Pluto 1980, table 3, p. 12.
4. Mandel *op. cit.* table 9, p. 28.
5. Independent Treasury Economic Model Club forecast, *Guardian* 13/10/80.
6. E. Mandel, *Late Capitalism*, London: New Left Books 1975, p. 137–38.
7. For a detailed discussion of the controversy between the two see Richard Day, 'Trotsky versus Kondratieff', *New Left Review* no. 99.
8. N. D. Kondratieff, 'The world economy and its conjuncture during and after the war', *Vologda* 1922 p. 60–61; quoted in Day *op. cit.* p. 76.
9. Day *op. cit.* p. 77.
10. Quoted in Day *op. cit.* p. 71.
11. Bob Rowthorn, 'Mandel's *Late Capitalism*', *New Left Review*, no. 98 p. 62.
12. *ibid.* p. 63.
13. Arghiri Emmanuel, *Unequal Exchange,* London: New Left Books, Chapter 3.
14. Mandel, *Marxist Economic Theory*, London: Merlin Press 1962, p. 453–59.
15. Mandel, *Late Capitalism, op. cit.*
16. *ibid.*
17. *ibid.* p. 159.
18. *ibid.* p. 179.
19. Caves and Krause (eds.), *Britain's Economic Performance*, Washington: Brookings 1980, p. 185.
20. See in particular: Guerin, *Fascism and Big Business*, London: Pathfinder Press 1973, and Trotsky, *The Struggle Against Fascism In Germany*, Harmondsworth: Penguin 1975.

2 The Changing Shape of the Working Class pages 46–66

1. OECD, *Labour Force Statistics*, Paris: OECD 1974.
2. OECD, *Labour Force Statistics 1957–1968*, Paris: OECD 1970, graph 6.
3. International Labour Office *Yearbooks* for the period.
4. OECD, *op. cit.*
5. See E. Mandel, *op. cit.* p. 336.
6. Ann D. Morgan, in *Deindustrialisation*, edited F. T. Blackaby, London, Heinemann 1979, tables 1 and 2.
7. Berbeogh and Landsberg, 'Transnational production and the world wide control of advanced capitalism', *CSE Conference Paper*, London 1979, no. 34.

8. *Committee to Review the Functioning of Financial Institutions*, London: HMSO 1980, table 42.
9. M. Barratt Brown, *From Labourism to Socialism,* Nottingham: Spokesman Books 1972, table 4.7.
10. G. Minnerup, 'West Germany since the war', *New Left Review* no. 99, p. 15.
11. Chitoshi Yanaga, 'The Role of the Bureaucracy' in *Japan Reader 2*, edited by J. Livingston, J. Moore, F. Oldfather, Harmondsworth: Penguin 1976, p. 415.
12. J. Livingston, J. Moore, F. Oldfather, *op. cit.* p. 430.
13. D. S. Landes, *The Unbound Prometheus*, London: Cambridge University Press 1970, pp. 531–32.
14. H. Braverman, *Labour and Monopoly Capital*, New York: Monthly Review Press 1974, pp. 170–71.
15. OECD, *Labour Force Statistics 1960–1971*, Paris: OECD.
16. K. Marx, *Capital* Vol. 1, *op. cit.,* p. 918.
17. CIS, 'Women Under Attack', Report no. 15, London: CIS 1977.
18. General Household Survey Unit, *The Changing Circumstances of Women 1971–76*, London: OPCS August 1979.
19. Irene Bruegel; 'Women as a reserve army of labour: a note on recent British experience', *Feminist Review*, no. 3 1979.
20. E. P. Thompson, *The Making of the English Working Class*, Harmondsworth: Penguin 1968, pp. 343 and 469–81.
21. Marx and Engels, *On Colonialism*, Moscow: Progress Publishers 1960, p. 301.
22. Castles and Kosack, *Immigrant Workers and Class Structure in Western Europe*, London: Oxford University Press 1973, pp. 112–13.
23. Source: OECD statistics for 1975.
24. Irene Bruegel, *op. cit.* footnote 14, p. 21.
25. See Jenny Hurstfield's excellent *The Part Time Trap* for a fuller analysis of these trends. London: Low Pay Unit, 1979.
26. *Guardian*, 5/12/78.
27. The *OECD Observer*, no. 90, January 1978.

3. The Regional Dynamic pages 67–90

1. W. Hannington, *Unemployed Struggles 1919–36,* London: Lawrence & Wishart 1977, p. 309.
2. See E. Mandel, *Marxist Economic Theory*, London: Merlin, 1968, Chapter 4.
3. E. Mandel, *Late Capitalism*, London, New Left Books 1975, pp. 86–89.
4. Pollard, *The Development of the British Economy 1914–1950*, London: Arnold 1962, p. 114.
5. Pollard, *op. cit.* p. 126.
6. See *The Royal Commission on the Distribution of the Industrial Population*, London: HMSO 1940.
7. See. E. Mandel, *Late Capitalism*, *op. cit.* Chapter 7.
8. Manufacturing employment since 1970 has declined by 12 per cent in the middle Atlantic states (a division of the north-east) but increased by 7 per cent in the south Atlantic states. For internal migration within the US see *New Statesman* 3/10/80.
9. More than a million people between the ages of 15 and 45 moved into the South-East region between 1923 and 1938.
10. P. Hall, *Urban and Regional Planning*, Harmondsworth: Penguin 1975, table 2.
11. Location of Offices Bureau, *Statistical Handbook*, 1975.
12. P. Hall *op. cit.* table 4.
13. Of the £600 million in capital grants allocated prior to 1976, £210 million was for chemical plant. *Guardian*, 12/10/78.
14. August Graziono Mezzogiorno, *Cambridge Journal of Economics*, no. 2, 1978, pp. 353–72.
15. *Financial Times*, 16/1/79.
16. *Second Report of CEC Regional Development Incentives*, London: HMSO, 1974.
17. A 1978 study by investment consultants Plan Location International compared the incentives on offer for investment in the EEC countries. Four types of investment, employing different ratios of capital and labour were analysed: in three out of the four types, Northern Ireland came first, in the other, second to Ireland.
18. *The Times*, 19/11/78.
19. *Department of Employment Gazette*, January 1980, p. 9.

4. London—The Urban Dynamic pages 91–120

1. Manpower Services Unit, *Employment in the Metropolitan Conurbations*, Department of Employment 1978, Table 1.
2. P. Hall, *The Industries of London Since 1861,* London: Hutchinson 1962, table 1.
3. Knight, Tsapatsaris and Jaroszek, *GLC Research Memorandum No. 501.*
4. Robert Dennis, 'The decline of manufacturing employment in Greater London', *Urban Studies 15*, pp. 63–73, in particular table V.
5. Manpower Services Unit, *op. cit.* table 13.

6. Liverpool City Planning Officer, 'Unemployment in Liverpool', *Report to City Council*, 1980, CPO/257/80 table 6; Merseyside Socialist Research Group, *Merseyside in Crisis*, fig. 2.
7. Joint Docklands Action Group, *Jobs—The Way Forward*, 1978, p. 16.
8. Fullerton, *The Development of British Transport Networks*, London: OUP 1975, pp. 30–38.
9. Colin Sparks, 'Fascism and the working class', table 4, *International Socialism* 2:3.
10. Locational Attitudes Group Survey, *Minutes of Evidence*, Commons Expenditure Committee, July 1973, HMSO.
11. *Urban Studies*, no. 15, pp. 268–73.
12. *Economist* 1/1/77, p. 20.
13. Dennis *op. cit.* table 3.
14. CDP pamphlets contain many local studies with examples in these different categories; see also *Tottenham's Future Jobs—Who Decides?* Tottenham Employment Group 1979.
15. Knight *op. cit.* as note 3.
16. *NEDO Industrial Review* to 1977—Clothing.
17. Les Levidow, 'Grunwick: technology and class struggle', *Radical Science Journal* 6/7.
18. See Rosa Luxemburg, *Social Reform or Revolution*, London: Merlin Press, p. 25; Mandel, *Late Capitalism*, Chapter 8; Braverman, *Labour and Monopoly Capital*, pp. 155–67.
19. Herbert Brochier, 'Principal characteristics of small firms', in ed. Livingston *et al, Japan Reader 2*, Harmondsworth: Penguin, 1976, pp. 422–23.
20. Victoria Goddard, 'Domestic industry in Naples', *Critique of Anthropology*, No. 9/10, Vol. 3, 1977; Mandel, *Late Capitalism*, p. 535, note 17.
21. *Hackney People's Press*, August 1980.
22. GLC Minutes 7.2.79. *Report of Planning Committee*, Office of Development and Employment.
23. *Built Environment*, October 1972 p. 445.
24. Location of Offices Bureau, *Case Studies of Decentralised Firms*, 1977, pp. 9–10.
25. Location of Offices Bureau, *Statistics Handbook* (1975) and *Annual Report* (1978).
26. Jane Barker and Hazel Downing, 'Office automation, word-processing and the transformation of patriarchal relations', *Conference of Socialist Economists*, Annual Conference Papers, *pp. 13–18; see also* CIS, *The New Technology*, Report no. 23, 1979.
27. James O'Connor, *The Fiscal Crisis of the State*, New York: St. Martin's Press 1973, pp. 5–10; 51–54.
28. Barker and Downing, *op. cit.* p. 18.
29. Harry Braverman, *Labour and Monopoly Capital*, New York: Monthly Review Press, 1974, p. 277.
30. *Thames Report*, Thames TV, 2/10/80; other figures British Tourist Authority.
31. For a full analysis and excellent discussion of London's hotel and catering industries see Liz Dronfield and Paul Soto, in CIS, *Hardship Hotel*, Report no. 27, 1980.
32. Deakin, Earl and Thompson, 'Assessing London's social problems', GLC Policy Studies and Intelligence Branch 1977, p. 7.
33. Information from GLC Policy Studies and Intelligence Branch.
34. Information from Lambeth CRC.
35. Liverpool City Planning Officer, *op. cit.*
36. Gareth Stedman Jones, *Outcast London. op. cit.*
37. Two books that give an insight into London politics at the time are: E. P. Thompson, *William Morris—Romantic to Revolutionary*, London: Merlin Press 1977; and Yvonne Kapp, *Eleanor Marx*, Vol. 2, London: Lawrence & Wishart, 1976.

5. The Fragmented Family pages 121–145

1. N. J. Smelsner, *The Industrial Revolution and the British Working Class Family: Essays in Sociological Explanation*, New York: Random House 1968.
2. Rosser and Harris, *The Family and Social Change*, London: Routledge & Kegan Paul 1965, pp. 8–10.
3. See Young and Willmott, *The Symmetrical Family*, Harmondsworth: Penguin 1971 and M. Anderson, *Family Structure in 19th Century Lancashire*, London: Cambridge University Press 1971.
4. Irene Bruegel, 'The State of the Family', in *International Socialism*, Vol. 2, No. 1, London 1978.
5. The most notable exception being the Lancashire textile workers.
6. *Women Take Issue*, London: Hutchinson 1978, p. 23.
7. Amrit Wilson, *Finding a Voice: Asian Women in Britain*, London: Virago 1978, pp. 31–42.
8. Mark Abrams, *Beyond Three Score and Ten*, London: Age Concern 1978.
9. P. Townsend, *The Family Life of Old People*, Harmondsworth: Penguin 1963, p. 33.
10. Mark Abrams, *op. cit.* table 17.
11. Richard Leete, *Population Trends*, no. 13, London: OPCS, Autumn 1978.
12. *What Chance a Home?*, London: Catholic Housing Aid Society, figure 4.
13. Elsa Ferri, *Growing Up in a One Parent Family*, Harmondsworth: Penguin 1968, p. 147.

14. A major survey of GLC lettings found that in the inter-war unmodernised flats and the pre-1919 flats there were nearly three times as many blacks as whites; and that 'other social groups disproportionately found in older flats include the homeless, the unskilled and female single parent families.' From a report (17/11/76) by Director of Housing Management and Maintenance and drawn from *GLC Research Report*, no. 21: 'Colour and allocation of GLC housing' by John Parker and Keith Dugmore.

15. See Susan Brownmiller, *Against Our Will*, Harmondsworth: Penguin 1977, pp. 182, 185, and 349.

16. *Woman's Own*, 16/3/79.

17. George W. Brown and Tirril Harris, *Social Origins of Depression*, London: Tavistock 1978, p. 151.

18. Dennis Marsden, *Mothers Alone*, Harmondsworth: Penguin, 1973, table 8, p. 350.

19. Ian Gough, *The Political Economy of the Welfare State*, London: Macmillan, 1978, Chapter 4.

20. London-Edinburgh Weekend Return Group, *In and Against the State*, London: Pluto 1980.

21. *Profiles of the Elderly 4*, London, Age Concern.

22. There was a 30 per cent decline in the commercial sector's provision of hostel beds between 1965 and 1972 (*Hostels and Lodgings for Single People*, London, OPCS, p. 16).

23. Between 1965 and 1972 only 7 new local authority hostels, containing 359 beds were built. OPCS, *op. cit.*

24. *Evening Standard*, 4/12/78.

25. *Sunday Times*, 27/11/77.

26. Margaret Wynn, *Family Policy*, Harmondsworth: Penguin, 1971, p. 25.

27. *See, Who Cares?*, London: National Children's Bureau, 1978.

28. 'Children in care of local authorities', 31/3/75, *DHSS Personal Social Services Local Authority Statistics*, A/F 75/12.

29. From 1972 to 1975 the number of children who were taken into care because a local authority judged their parents had 'persistently failed to discharge' their obligations rendering them unfit to care for their children, increased by 30 per cent.

30. S. Baxter, unpublished M.Med Sci thesis. University of Nottingham 1978.

31. See paper by Janet Headley, 'Population control, racism and imperialism', and 'Depo Provera: a case study'. Wendy Savage, 'The use of Depo Provera in East London'. *Fertility and Contraception*, Vol. 2, no. 3, July 1978.

32. M. N. Caulfield, *Socialist Revolution*, special issue on the family, San Francisco, 1977.

6. From Consent to Coercion pages 146–174

1. From 'Time Come' by Linton Kwesi Johnson in *Dread, Beat & Blood*, London, Bogle l'Ouverture Press, 1978.

2. S. Hall *et al*, *Policing the Crisis*, London: Macmillan, 1978, p. 217.

3. S. Hall, 'Drifting into a law and order society', Cobden Trust Human Rights Day Lecture, 1979.

4. *Report of the Committee of Inquiry into Police Interrogation Procedures in Northern Ireland*, HMSO, Cmnd. 7497, 1979.

5. Peter Chalk, Surveillance, the Law and Military Rule.

6. Granada TV, *World in Action*, 'The Police and the Public', 8/4/80.

7. *Sunday Times*, 6/4/80.

8. *Observer*, 6/4/80.

9. *Sunday Times*, 6/4/80.

10. A. Sivanandan, 'Race, Class and the State', *Race and Class*, Vol. XVII 1976, p. 364.

11. *Police Against Black People*, Institute of Race Relations evidence to Select Committee on Criminal Procedure, Spring 1979, p. 14.

12. Derek Humphry, *Police Power and Black Power*, Harmondsworth: Penguin, p. 209.

13. A. Sivanandan, *op. cit.* p. 361.

14. *Race Today*, interview, April 1975.

15. S. Hall *et al*, *op. cit.* p. 351.

16. Jerry White, 'Campbell Bunk—a lumpen community in London between the wars', *History Workshop Journal*, no. 8, 1979.

17. The phrase used by Commander Randall, Lewisham police, in October 1975.

18. Select Committee on Race Relations and Immigration, *Minutes of Evidence 1975–76 Session*, HMSO, p. 178.

19. *Evening Standard* 31/8/76.

20. *Guardian* 6/4/79.

21. *Guardian* 7/4/79.

22. McNee, 'Crime and the young', *Police Journal*, Vol. 11, no. 1.

23. *Observer* 1/7/79—report of NYB submission to Royal Commission on Criminal Procedure.

24. 'A Cause for Alarm', A study of policing in Lambeth, ALARM 1979, p. 31.

25. *New Statesman*, 21/6/79.

26. Peter Kandler, letter to the *Guardian* 9/1/80.

27. See Brian Rose-Smith's essay in *Policing the Police*, Vol. 1, ed. Peter Hain, London: John Calder 1979.
28. *Leveller* p. 12, July 1979.
29. Sir Charles Rowan quoted in *Police Studies*, Vol. 1, no. 3, p. 17.
30. Ackroyd, Margolis, Rosenhead and Shallice, *Technology of Political Control*, London: Pluto 1980, p. 132.
31. See in particular the publication *State Research*.
32. *Science for the People*, no. 37, p. 3.
33. F. E. C. Gregory, 'Changes in the American system of policing since 1960', p. 362, *Police Journal*, Vol. 21, no. 4.
34. S. Hall, Cobden Trust Lecture *op. cit.*
35. Ackroyd *et al, op. cit.* p. 203.
36. 'Whose law and order?' Campaign Against A Criminal Trespass Law, 1979, p. 6.
37. See Antonio Gramsci, 'State and civil society', *Selections from the Prison Notebooks*, London: Lawrence & Wishart 1971.
38. *Daily Telegraph*, 9/7/80.
39. See 'Mersey Police Chief attacks press' *Guardian*, 23/5/80; 'Police Chief accuses Clergy of meddling', *Guardian*, 24/8/79; 'Scathing attack on police critics', *Guardian*, 22/5/80.
40. *Report of the Commissioners of Police of the Metropolis* for 1977, Cmnd 7238 HMSO, p. 5.
41. S. Hall *et al, op. cit.* p. 14.
42. Mark, *In the Office of Constable*, London: Collins 1978, p. 244.

Conclusion: New Unities and Alliances pages 175–186

1. See Stuart Holland, *Beyond Capitalist Planning*, London: OUP 1978 and by the same author, *The Socialist Challenge*, London: Quartet 1975 and also, *Strategy for Socialism*, Nottingham: Spokesman 1975.
2. Many articles have appeared dealing with different varieties of the Alternative Economic Strategy. See in particular Alan Freeman, 'The Alternative Economic Strategy: a critique', *International*, Vol. 5, no. 2, London 1980 and the debate in the issues of *International Socialism* from Vol. 2, no. 6 to Vol. 2, no. 8.
3. K. Marx, 'Letter to Bracke', 5 May 1875, quoted in Sue Cockerill, 'Replay to left reformism', *International Socialism*, Vol. 2, no. 8, London 1980, p. 101.
4. For a discussion of this idea see London-Edinburgh Weekend Return Group, *In And Against the State*, London: Pluto Press 1980, Chapter 6.

Index

126, 132ff; and part time work, 62; and motherhood, 127; and sexual violence, 133; and unemployment, 62; in the workforce, 57, 62, 82, 95, 96, 106, 108, 110–111